THE HERBAL PANTRY

THE
HERBAL
PANTRY

EMELIE TOLLEY AND CHRIS MEAD

CLARKSON POTTER/PUBLISHERS
NEW YORK

Published by Clarkson N. Potter, Inc., 201 East 50th Street, New York, New York 10022.
Member of the Crown Publishing Group.

CLARKSON N. POTTER, POTTER, and colophon are trademarks of Clarkson N. Potter, Inc.

Manufactured in Japan

Book design by Jane Treuhaft

LIBRARY OF CONGRESS CATALOGING-IN-PUBLICATION DATA
Tolley, Emelie.
The herbal pantry / Emelie Tolley and Chris Mead.—1st ed.
p.   cm.
Includes index.
1. Cookery (Herbs).   2. Herbs.   I. Chris Mead.   II. Title.
TX819.H4T64   1992
641.6 ' 57—dc20   92-9471
CIP
ISBN 0-517-58331-3
10 9 8 7 6 5 4 3 2

*To my
patient friends…
and to Chris,
who always
manages
to make things
beautiful.*

—ET

*To Emelie,
Mary, family,
and friends.*

—CM

ur thanks to everyone—family, friends, and famous and not-so-famous chefs and gardeners—who has ever cooked us a meal or shared a knowledge of herbs and gardening. Each of them in some way has been an inspiration for this book. We are grateful, too, to Patti and Jeffrey Kenner, Tonin MacCallum, Robert Kinnaman, and Brian Ramaekers for so generously letting us photograph in their homes, and to Myra Oram for always coming to the rescue when we need her. ❧ We would also like to thank Jane Treuhaft and Howard Klein for designing this book with so much sensitivity and talent, making our vision reality; and Pam Krauss, our editor, for her unwavering support and intelligent editorial guidance. And our thanks, too, to all our friends at Clarkson Potter who do so much to take our ideas, make them into books, and then make them successful.

∾ INTRODUCTION

After the long winter, I welcome the first days of spring. The warm sun soon coaxes a few green shoots up through the rich soil of my herb garden and it isn't long before I can savor the sprightly taste of fresh herbs whenever the mood strikes me. Blades of chives always seem to appear in time to make the first asparagus even tastier, but this is just the beginning of the season's bounty. Here on the eastern end of Long Island, we're surrounded by an abundance of fresh produce all summer long. Gardens flourish and farm stands and markets are piled high with just-picked fruits and vegetables, freshly caught fish, country eggs and chickens, and so many bunches of lush herbs that even those without a garden of their own can enjoy wonderful herbal flavor in everything from cold soups to fresh fruit compotes.

Unfortunately the climate here in the Northeast doesn't allow year-round gardening, so as the days grow shorter with the approach of fall, I start thinking about ways to prolong the tastes of summer. Freezing and drying part of my herb harvest for the bleak months ahead is the first step, but over the years I've discovered other interesting ways to incorporate the taste of fresh herbs into tasty treats that can be kept on the

∾ **Herbs add distinction to jellies, pickles, and preserves.**

pantry shelf or in the freezer. I might enliven orange marmalade with the sharp pungency of rosemary or make a spicy basil jelly to serve with chicken; flavor a fruity raspberry liqueur with rose geranium; add the special flavor of dill to mustard; sharpen a chutney with thyme; or enhance honey with lavender. Herbs give syrups, pickles, vinegars, oils, butters, olives, teas, and other condiments an added fillip, too.

Unlike my grandmother, who pickled and preserved out of

necessity, I do so purely for the pleasure of having something special to offer my family and friends. If you prepare just a few jars of jelly, a chutney, or a lovely liqueur whenever you have a few extra minutes, it's an enjoyable task rather than a tedious chore. Done in manageable batches, even water-processing is simple. And it's both comforting and satisfying when summer ends to see the pantry shelves stacked high with jars of tasty jellies, tangy mustards, pungent chutneys, and appetizing pickles; to have the freezer packed with herb-flavored butters; and the bar stocked with an array of luscious liqueurs, all subtly flavored with the herbs from my garden. I know they'll be there to help me create magic in the kitchen or to bestow on friends whenever I want to give a gift of love, and as I wrap these homemade gifts at holiday time I relive the pleasure of making them and look forward to sharing the flavors of my garden.

It's been enormous fun experimenting with different herbs to create the recipes in this book. Chris and I tasted endless variations; you'll find our favorites here along with master recipes, and a few ideas on how to use the finished products. Once you've tried the suggestions in this book, we hope you will explore different combinations of herbs to find those that suit your own particular tastes and needs best. We know you will enjoy the doing as well as the eating.

∾ **To dry herbs from your garden for herbal blends, tie them in small bunches at the stem end, then hang them upside down from a rack, ceiling beam, or even a hanger in a well-ventilated spot.**

～ THE BASICS

Whether you are making jams and jellies, pickles, mustards, or even liqueurs, there are a few basic rules that you must follow to ensure that the foods you preserve do not spoil. No matter what you are preserving, it is vitally important that all your equipment and the jars you plan to use be absolutely clean, with no bacteria lingering to taint the food.

Sugar, salt, vinegar, oil, and alcohol are to some degree natural preservatives. In some cases they will be adequate protection against spoilage. But if the recipe calls for small amounts of these ingredients, the fruits and vegetables you are working with are especially fragile, or you expect to keep the food for some time before using it, it's wise to process the jars in a hot-water bath. Freezing or refrigerating are other alternatives.

Here are a few tips on the best ways to proceed:

* Start with fresh, high-quality ingredients that are in good condition, and follow cooking directions precisely.
* Sterilize jars by boiling them for 10 minutes. Cover the jar tops and rubber rings with water, bring to a simmer, and turn off the heat. Let the jars and tops sit in the hot water until you are ready to use them, then drain them on a clean towel.
* To process the finished products in a hot-water bath, fill a large pot fitted with a rack half full of water and bring to a simmer. Lower the jars onto the rack, leaving some space between them, and add more boiling water if needed so the water covers the jars by 1 inch. Cover and bring to a boil, and process according to the size of the jars, generally 5 minutes for a half-pint or pint jar, 10 minutes for a quart. (If a recipe gives different processing times, follow the recipe.) The bath destroys the rings' elasticity; use new rings each time.
* Always label the finished product with the contents and the date.

～ OPPOSITE: **Emelie harvests herbs at the height of flavor from her herb border. ABOVE: A jar of tangy sweet cucumber pickles.**

I

JAMS AND JELLIES

<c ABOVE: **A selection of herbal jams and jellies.** OPPOSITE: **Briny pickled eggs.**

When making jellies, don't double or triple the recipe; if you do, it will require longer cooking, which may alter the balance of the natural pectin, sugar, and acid in the fruit, or cause the sugar to caramelize or burn. Remember that the less ripe the fruit is, the more pectin it contains, so always include a little fruit that is not fully ripened. Only a few fruits—apples, citrus fruits, currants, sour plums—have enough natural pectin to set; others require adding fresh apple juice or commercial pectin.

If there's too little acid in the fruit, the sugar in the jam may crystallize, so lemon juice is often added. Overcooking can also make the sugar crystallize. If this happens, reheat the jelly and add a little water and lemon juice, then return it to the jars.

It is impossible to set an exact cooking time for jellies and jams. The ripeness of the fruit, its acidity, and the amount of juice it contains will all have an effect. The jelly is done when a candy thermometer registers 220° F. or when a small amount dropped on a cold plate sets enough to hold the mark made when the tip of a spoon is pulled through it.

Pour the finished jelly into the clean jars to within ¼ inch of the top. Wipe any jelly from the rim and the edges with a clean towel. Immediately screw on the lids and process the jars in a hot-water bath for 5 to 10 minutes, depending on the size of the jar. Jams, jellies, and marmalades kept in glasses or jars without tops should be covered with a thin layer of paraffin. Pour the melted paraffin over jams and marmalades while they are hot; allow jelly to cool first. (While the jelly is cooling, cover it with a clean towel to keep it dust-free and avoid condensation.)

PICKLES

The acid in vinegar prevents the formation of bacteria, but since fruits and vegetables contain water which can dilute it to the point of being ineffective, it is best to try to eliminate some of this water before pickling. The two most common methods of accomplishing this are blanching the vegetables or covering them with coarse salt to draw out some of the water. If raw fruits or vegetables are marinated in the vinegar, it might be wise to drain the vinegar off and boil it after a day or so to evaporate some of the water. Also remember that wine vinegar, while mellower tasting than white vinegar, is also less acidic. To be absolutely sure that pickles remain safe to eat, it is best to process them in a hot-water bath. If the tops of any jars are bulging, discard them immediately, as this is a sign that bacteria have spoiled the food.

Foods preserved in oil will remain fresh for 3 to 6 months if the food is completely covered and they are stored in the refrigerator. However, with fragile foods such as mushrooms, or for prolonged storage, it is wise to process them in a hot-water bath first.

VINEGARS and OILS

People have been seasoning food with vinegars and olive oil for at least five thousand years. Although vinegar was probably discovered accidentally in prehistoric times when the yeasts in air caused the sugar in a juice or honey water to ferment, man has been assiduously cultivating  olives for their flavorful oil on the eastern edge of the Mediterranean since Neolithic times. Both are indispensable kitchen staples that add a lovely richness or tang to whatever they touch, and are even more delightful when a few herbs lend their pungent goodness. ❧

VINEGARS

Flavored vinegars are a simple way to add zest to salads, sauces, marinades, even desserts. And they imbue whatever you're cooking with added flavor without the addition of any fat, sugar, or salt. You can flavor a vinegar with a single herb or with a complex bouquet that might include citrus or spices along with a tasty mélange of herbs from the garden. Pungent herbs such as thyme, savory, sage, and rosemary are particularly good for meats; and while fennel and dill are traditionally used with fish, the lemony herbs such as lemon balm and lemon thyme as well as tarragon and basil are interesting alternatives that also complement chicken. Tarragon vinegar has long been used to enliven salads, but so can vinegars of basil, marjoram, or any herbs you might ordinarily toss into the salad bowl, including faintly cucumber-flavored borage blossoms or salad burnet, peppery nasturtiums, or oniony chive blossoms. I generally save the sweeter vinegars made from mint, rose, or lavender for fruit salads and desserts, where just a touch can be substituted for a dash of liqueur to heighten the fruit's own delightful flavor.

Just as there are different herbs to choose from, a variety of vinegars can serve as your base: cider vinegar, red or white wine vinegar, rice wine vinegar, and white vinegar. Distilled white vinegar and rice wine vinegars are the only ones that are perfectly colorless, but the former's taste is a bit sharp, so unless you're set

In a few short hours, with just a few simple ingredients, you can stock your pantry with vinegars.

on having a beautifully colored vinegar made from opal basil, borage, or chive blossoms at the expense of taste, save white vinegar for pickling and use white wine vinegar or the slightly sweet but very mild rice wine vinegar instead. Blending the two is another alternative. White wine vinegar is perhaps the most versatile of all, lending itself equally well to single herbs or combinations. Red wine vinegar seems more appropriate for the most pungent herbs, and cider vinegar for mint, dill, and basil. Whichever vinegar you choose, however, be sure it is of the finest quality. Even herbs can't make a harsh vinegar smooth.

Simple herb vinegars can be made from any culinary herb. Some of the best are:

- *Chives and chive blossoms.* The blossoms lend a beautiful mauve color. Use any time you want a hint of onion.
- *Dill* for fish and potato and other vegetable salads and marinades. The blossom is a pretty addition.
- *Salad burnet* or *borage* for a slight cucumber flavor. Borage flowers give the vinegar a lovely blue color.
- *Mint* for lamb and for fruit salads and desserts. Use any of the many varieties.
- *Sage* in red wine vinegar for marinades for fatty meats.
- *Lavender, elderflower, violet, scented geranium* or *rose* for desserts, fruits.
- *Nasturtium* flowers and leaves for anything that needs a peppery lift.
- *Tarragon* for salads and chicken dishes.
- *Fennel* for fish dishes or wherever you want a touch of anise.
- *Basil* for tomatoes, pasta salads, vegetable salads. *Opal basil* makes a handsomely tinted pink vinegar.

Any of these can be mixed together with other herbs such as thyme, rosemary, parsley, chervil, or marjoram, and with citrus zest, spices, or garlic. Generally a ratio of 1 cup of fresh or ⅓ cup dried herbs to 1 quart of vinegar works well. Try the recipes here, then experiment with blends that are particularly suited to the foods you like to cook.

There are two basic methods for making herb vinegar; the ingredients are the same for either. The recipes that follow make 1 quart.

METHOD ONE: Place the herbs (and citrus or spices if you are using them) in a large jar or bottle and pour the vinegar over them. Set the bottle in a sunny window for two weeks, turning it regularly. The heat of the sun will extract the flavor from the herbs. If you are planning to use the vinegar immediately, there is no need to filter it. However, if you plan to keep it for more than a few months before using or want to make a more handsome presentation, strain out the herbs and pour the vinegar through a coffee filter and into a clean bottle. Add one or two fresh sprigs of the herb or herbs used in the vinegar. They are especially pretty when they are in flower.

METHOD TWO: Place the herbs in a large jar or bottle. In a saucepan, heat the vinegar to the boiling point, remove from the flame, and pour over the herbs. Let steep until cool. Strain (the hot vinegar wilts the herbs) and bottle with one or two fresh sprigs as above.

For gifts or your own pleasure, strain finished vinegars and pour into pretty bottles, adding a sprig or two of fresh herbs.

PROVENCAL VINEGAR

With all the pungent flavors of Provence, this vinegar is excellent for meat marinades or in a robust dressing for vine-ripe tomato or eggplant salads.

1 sprig rosemary
1 sprig thyme
2 bay leaves
2 sprigs marjoram
1 sprig savory (optional)
1 sprig lavender
2 garlic cloves
1 small hot red pepper
1 quart white wine vinegar

SPICY LIME VINEGAR

This would be delicious in a chicken or fruit salad, as a marinade for chicken or lamb, or in a hollandaise for asparagus. Try it with lemon or orange zest, too.

4 sprigs mint
1 garlic clove
Zest of 1 lime
1 tablespoon coriander seeds
1 quart white wine vinegar

☙ LEFT: **Nasturtium, thyme flower, rose, and lavender vinegars are as pretty as they are tasty. RIGHT: Cucumber mousse with Zesty Dill Vinegar-marinated cucumbers.**

SALAD BOUQUET VINEGAR

This vinegar would enhance the vinaigrette for any green salad.

2 sprigs marjoram
2 sprigs salad burnet
1 sprig thyme
2 sprigs tarragon
2 sprigs parsley
5 chive blades
1 quart white wine vinegar

ZESTY DILL VINEGAR

For fish dishes, salads, potatoes, or cucumbers.

1 small bunch dill
1 or 2 dill blossoms
Zest of 1 lemon
1 garlic clove
1 tablespoon mustard seeds
1 quart white wine vinegar

ITALIAN COUNTRY VINEGAR

Use this for mixed green salads with shavings of fresh Parmesan cheese, on sliced tomatoes, and in marinades for veal, pork, or beef.

2 sprigs rosemary
4 sprigs oregano
1 sprig sage
3 small stems basil
2 sprigs parsley
1 garlic clove
1 tablespoon black peppercorns
1 quart red wine vinegar

COUNTRY SPINACH SALAD

1 pound fresh spinach
 Leaves from 1 generous bunch basil,
  about 2 cups
1 small sweet red onion, thinly sliced
3 beets, cooked and sliced
1 cup shaved Parmesan cheese
4 slices prosciutto, julienned
1 cup walnut halves

VINAIGRETTE
2 tablespoons Italian Country Vinegar
1 teaspoon Quick Herbed Mustard
 flavored with basil (page 100)
6 tablespoons olive oil
 Salt and pepper to taste

Wash the spinach carefully in several changes of water. Dry well, tear into manageable pieces, and combine in a salad bowl with the washed basil leaves. Scatter the onion, beets, cheese, prosciutto, and walnuts over the top.

Place the vinegar and mustard in a bowl and whisk in the oil until well blended. Season with salt and pepper to taste. Pour the dressing over the salad and toss well.

SERVES 4 TO 6

❧ **A touch of lusty Italian Country Vinegar heightens the flavor of this hearty salad.**

OILS

Flavored oils are just as versatile as vinegars. I use them to season salads; spice up marinades; add savor to grilled or sautéed foods; flavor cheeses; and enliven sauces. Some, with the addition of chopped herbs and cheese, are flavorful enough to act as a fast and simple pasta sauce.

Just as with vinegars, the possible variations are endless. However, since oils tend to become rancid once opened, they cannot be stored in the pantry indefinitely as vinegars can. It is best to make them in smaller quantities or settle for just one or two different flavors, letting your choice reflect the foods and tastes you prefer. If you grill a lot of meats, you might decide on an oil perfumed with all the aromatic herbs of Provence; stir-fried foods might suggest an oil flavored with star anise, cilantro, garlic, ginger, and chives; Southwestern cooking, one with chilies, cilantro, cumin seed, and garlic. In the summer I often keep a bottle of basil oil handy to use with ripe tomatoes, dill or fennel oil for grilling fish, and fiery chili pepper oil to add heat to anything.

Although olive oil contributes its own taste to these oils, peanut or vegetable oils can be substituted if you prefer a less assertive taste.

Any oil can be flavored simply with a single herb or with a complex mixture of herbs, spices, and citrus. Incorporate your favorite seasonings in a ratio of 1 cup of herbs or other flavorings to 1 quart of oil. If you use garlic, remove it after 2 weeks, or it will overpower the other flavors. Make sure all the ingredients are completely covered with oil, or mold will develop. To avoid any problems, strain the herbs out after they have had time to flavor the oil, about 2 weeks. Here are just a few of the possible combinations. Each makes 1 quart of flavored oil.

∾ OPPOSITE: **Fast and easy to make, herb oils can be flavored with any combination of herbs and spices. ABOVE: Grilled vegetables benefit from a basting of herbed oil.**

FABULOUS FISH OIL

For marinating and broiling fish and for fish salads.

3 dried fennel stalks
2 sprigs dill
3 sprigs lemon thyme
3 sprigs parsley
1 tablespoon coriander seeds
1 teaspoon black peppercorns
Zest of 1 lemon
1 quart olive oil

HERBES DE PROVENCE OIL

For marinating or sautéing grilled meats, or marinating cheeses.

3 sprigs rosemary
2 sprigs thyme
2 garlic cloves
3 sprigs marjoram
3 sprigs oregano
2 small stems basil
3 bay leaves
6 black peppercorns
1 quart olive or vegetable oil

∽ For a subtle, delicious flavor, marinate fish and vegetables in herbal oil, then use a brush made of herb sprigs to baste them as they grill; toss the brush onto the coals just before the fish is done.

SOUTHWESTERN OIL

For fajitas, chili, or anything you want to give a Southwestern twist.

    3 dried hot red peppers
    1 garlic clove
    1 small bunch cilantro
    1 teaspoon cumin seeds
    4 sprigs oregano
    1 quart vegetable or olive oil

PASTA OIL

Use this in pasta salads or add a few fresh herbs or tomatoes for a quick pasta sauce.

    3 sprigs sage
    2 garlic cloves
    1 small bunch parsley
    1 small hot red pepper
    5 ounces Parmesan cheese cut in small
       chunks
    1 quart extra-virgin olive oil

∾ LEFT: **Sautéeing beef, peppers, and onions for fajitas in Southwestern Oil infuses them with flavor. RIGHT: Sun-dried tomatoes, fresh sage, and Pasta Oil transform packaged tortellini into an impromptu salad.**

SPICY OIL

Use this in stir-fries or to marinate pork or chicken.

2 small hot dried chilies
2 garlic cloves
4 slices ginger root, ¼-inch thick
1 cinnamon stick
1 star anise pod
1 teaspoon coriander seeds
1 teaspoon whole allspice berries
  Zest of ½ orange
1 quart olive oil

THAI OIL

Use this to marinate or sauté chicken and beef or in cold beef or chicken salads.

3 lemon grass blades
2 small stems basil
4 sprigs coriander
2 sprigs mint
1 garlic clove
1 slice fresh ginger root, ⅛-inch thick
1 quart peanut oil

☙ RIGHT: **Crisply fried basil is an authentic garnish for Thai Chicken.**

CHICKEN WITH A TOUCH OF THAI

Note that this must marinate.

1 chicken, cut in serving pieces
½ cup Thai Oil
1 cup julienned basil
½ cup white wine
4 sprigs fresh mint, chopped
  Salt and pepper to taste

Wash and dry the chicken pieces. Place them in a single layer in a baking pan and brush generously on both sides with Thai Oil. Cover with plastic wrap; let stand for 2 hours at room temperature.

Put any remaining oil in a large skillet and heat over a medium-hot flame. Add the chicken pieces to the pan and brown on both sides. Lower the heat and continue to cook, turning occasionally, until the chicken is browned and cooked through, about 25 minutes.

Remove the chicken pieces from the pan, drain on paper towels, and set aside. Increase the heat and add a little more oil to the pan if necessary. When the oil is hot, add half the basil and fry quickly. Remove and drain on paper towels. Deglaze the pan with the wine. To serve, place the chicken pieces on a platter and pour the pan juices over them. Sprinkle with the fried basil, remaining fresh basil, and mint. Season to taste at the table.

SERVES 4

BUTTERS
and **HERBAL BLENDS**

If you use herbs to add extra flavor to the foods you serve, your reputation as a good cook is assured even if you serve nothing more complicated than a perfectly cooked omelet or a simple grilled chop. And you can easily take advantage of herbal flavors all through the year, even when a supply of fresh herbs isn't available. Simply keep your freezer stocked with a variety of herb butters made when the garden is at its prime and your pantry filled with pungent herbal seasoning blends ready to add zest to everything from vegetables to popcorn. ❧

HERB BUTTERS

Butter has been with us since ancient times and was probably first married to herbs during the Middle Ages, when it was wrapped in sorrel leaves and stored in earthenware pots filled with salted water. The purpose of this, of course, was to keep the butter sweet and fresh, but I'm sure the sorrel imparted some of its sharp lemony taste to the butter in the process.

Since keeping butter fresh is no longer a problem, busy cooks have creative freedom in choosing the herbs to flavor their butters. They can be blended to complement a particular dish: mint and chives for a tender lamb chop; fennel or tarragon for fish; rose geranium for toast or scones; basil, oregano, and garlic for a loaf of warm bread or a bowl of freshly cooked pasta. A versatile combination such as parsley, chives, and marjoram can be kept in the freezer and used to add last-minute flavor to almost anything.

The basic procedure for making herb butters is simple. The butter, preferably unsalted, is creamed until it is light and supple, then chopped herbs are stirred into it along with a little lemon juice and salt and pepper if desired. (The salt can be omitted with little loss of flavor by those on a salt-free diet.) For those worried about cholesterol, substitute margarine or one of the butter and margarine blends available in supermarkets. Herb flowers or seeds can be used in combination with or in place of the fresh or dried leaves.

For festive occasions, pack the soft butter into a wooden butter mold, chill until firm, then turn out with the imprint on top. Use candy molds to create interesting shapes or make balls or curls with butter paddles or a butter curler and heap them in a dish over a layer of cracked ice. Or you might roll the butter between two pieces of wax paper into a rectangle about ¼-inch thick, chill, and use cookie or canapé cutters to cut out hearts, flowers, or other suitable shapes. Simpler still, just pack the butter into an attractive dish with a cover or shape the butter into a cylinder, wrap it well, freeze, and cut off slices as you need them. Decorating the butter or the plate with herb sprigs or flowers makes it even more visually appealing.

◠ Use grooved paddles to roll herbal butters into attractive balls.

BASIC RECIPE

½ pound (2 sticks) unsalted butter
*5 tablespoons chopped fresh herbs
   and/or herb flowers or 5 teaspoons
   dried herbs or 2½ teaspoons
   herb seeds*
*1 teaspoon lemon juice or a few
   gratings of lemon zest (optional)
   Salt and white pepper to taste or dry
   mustard, paprika, cumin (optional)*

Chop the herbs very fine or pulverize the seeds. Cream the butter and blend in the herbs and seasonings. Shape as desired and chill or freeze up to 6 months.

MAKES 1/2 POUND

Suggested Combinations

- Dill, mustard seed, parsley, and a touch of lemon rind or a few mustard seeds for fish and potatoes.
- Thyme, garlic, chives, oregano, and parsley for tomatoes, zucchini, eggplant, or beef.
- Sage, parsley, and chives for chicken, veal, rice, and pasta.
- Tarragon or fennel, lemon zest, and parsley for fish, chicken, or eggs.
- Chives, mint, and chervil for fish, tomatoes, carrots, peas.

The traditional pairing of savory and beans is easily accomplished with an herb butter.

- Basil and garlic for lamb, chicken, or fish.
- Salad burnet, garlic chives, and parsley for potatoes, tomatoes, veal, salmon.
- Savory, marjoram, and parsley for beans, veal, beef, corn.
- Caraway seed and parsley for cabbage, carrots, potatoes, and bread.
- Aniseed, grated ginger, and orange zest for pork, chicken, or carrots.
- Cilantro, cumin, parsley, and dried red or fresh jalapeño pepper for a taste of the Southwest on rice, chicken, pork, potatoes, peas, or corn.
- Basil, tomato paste, and oregano for fish, chicken, pasta, and rice.
- Rosemary, chives, parsley, and garlic for potatoes, rice, pasta, beef, veal, chicken.
- Tarragon, chives, chervil, and white wine for fish, chicken, or eggs.
- Basil, thyme, and parsley for bread, vegetables, tuna, salmon, and shrimp.
- Anise hyssop, parsley, and chives for fish, chicken, veal.
- Mint, garlic, and parsley for lamb, mussels, swordfish, chicken, peas, carrots, green beans, or eggs.
- Rosemary, savory, thyme, oregano, marjoram, lavender, and garlic for grilled meats.
- Calendula petals, chives, and parsley for chicken, rice, or eggs.
- Scented geranium, rose, or pinks for toast, scones, waffles.

For a pretty presentation, cut herb butters into decorative shapes and garnish, OVERLEAF. Or wrap a block of butter in rose geranium leaves and let stand overnight to absorb their sweet flavor, BELOW.

ROAST PORK WITH SAGE FLOWER SAUCE

 1 bay leaf
 1 sprig thyme
 2 tablespoons Fines Herbes (page 35)
 1 shallot, chopped
 3 tablespoons olive oil
 6 tablespoons orange juice
   Salt and pepper to taste
 2½ to 3 pounds pork loin
 2 tablespoons Sage, Parsley, and
   Chive Butter made with sage
   flowers
   Sage flowers for garnish (optional)

Make a marinade with the herbs, shallot, oil, 4 tablespoons of the orange juice, and salt and pepper. Place in a large plastic bag and add the pork. Close tightly with a twist tie and marinate, turning occasionally, for at least 5 hours.

Preheat the oven to 400° F.

When ready to cook, discard the bay leaf and thyme sprig and place the pork and the remaining marinade in the center of a large piece of foil. Close securely, place in a roasting pan, and cook for 1½ hours or until the pork registers 160° F. on an instant meat thermometer.

Drain the pan juices into a saucepan and add the herb butter and the remaining 2 tablespoons of orange juice. Cook over medium heat until the butter is melted and the sauce has thickened slightly, about 10 minutes; keep warm. To serve, slice the roast, pour the sauce over it, and garnish with sage flowers if desired.

SERVES 4 TO 6

LEFT: **The sage blossoms that give the sauce for this pork roast pungency are also a handsome garnish.** ABOVE: **An old-fashioned wooden butter mold gives herb butters eye appeal.**

HERBAL BLENDS

At what point in time people discovered they could dry herbs and blend them into flavorful and healthful seasonings remains a mystery, but certainly by the Middle Ages amazing combinations of herbs and spices were used in noble kitchens throughout England. There are several theories as to why. Many people believe these exotic blends served to cover up the taste of foods, especially meats, that had gone a bit off. Their pungency would have helped, but perhaps our ancestors already knew what contemporary scientists researching how to eliminate chemical preservatives from food have discovered: rosemary and sage contain natural preservatives. Another theory holds that herbs and spices made palatable foods that had been boiled until almost tasteless. And, of course, the human desire for status was also a factor: only the wealthy could afford expensive Eastern spices.

Whatever the reason, over the years each nationality has developed a unique blend of seasonings that imparts a distinct ethnic flavor to its cuisine: *garam masala* in India, *fines herbes* and *bouquets garnis* in France, and *ras el-hanout* in Morocco, for example. And herbal mixes can also enhance specific foods such as fish, chicken, beef, or vegetables, while piquant blends of herbs such as savory, dill, thyme, and garlic can help cut down on salt and fat without eliminating taste. I like to put my favorite herbal seasoning in a pretty shaker and set it right on the table where it's as readily accessible as the salt and pepper. If you can't bear to give up salt altogether, dilute the salt on your table with an equal amount of herbs.

Herbal blends add interest to a variety of dishes at any time of the year and are especially handy when you're in a hurry. Since the pungency of

∽ ABOVE: **For best flavor, make blends from freshly dried herbs.** OPPOSITE: **To make a quick dip, stir your favorite herbal blend, chopped tomato, and minced jalapeño into sour cream or plain yogurt.**

any dried herb starts to dissipate after six months, mix up relatively small amounts and replace them once your garden is in bloom again. To keep them at their peak, store in a cool, dry, and dark place.

BOUQUET GARNI

This traditional French seasoning is used in soups and stews.

¼ cup dried parsley
4 bay leaves, crumbled
2 tablespoons dried thyme
2 tablespoons dried marjoram
2 tablespoons dried lovage leaves

Mix the herbs together. Place 1 tablespoon of the mixture in a small muslin bag or in the center of a 4-inch square of fine cheesecloth, doubled. Tie the bag or gather up the corners of the square and tie with a kitchen string, leaving a long end that can be tied to the handle of the pot so it is easily removed from the dish before serving. Store the bags in a jar with a tight-fitting lid.

MAKES ENOUGH FOR
10 TO 12 BAGS

⌒ No French cook would make a stew without the addition of a traditional bouquet garni.

FINES HERBES

Use this blend for omelets, soups, fish, butters, and vegetables.

2 tablespoons dried chervil
2 tablespoons dried chives
2 tablespoons dried tarragon
2 tablespoons dried parsley

Mix well and store in a jar.

MAKES ABOUT 1/2 CUP

ITALIAN SEASONING

Use on pizzas, pasta, herb bread—any dish that needs a hint of Italian flavor.

½ cup dried oregano
½ cup dried basil
¼ cup dried parsley
1 tablespoon fennel seeds, crushed
2 tablespoons dried sage
1 tablespoon hot red pepper flakes

Mix well and store in a jar.

MAKES ABOUT 1 1/2 CUPS

HERBES DE PROVENCE

Use for marinating and grilling meats.

¼ cup dried marjoram
¼ cup dried oregano
¼ cup dried savory
½ cup dried rosemary
½ cup dried thyme
2 tablespoons dried lavender leaves
2 tablespoons dried fennel seeds or
   stalks

Mix well and store in a jar.

MAKES ABOUT 2 CUPS

↬ **Herbes de Provence, a pungent blend of many provençal herbs including lavender, is unsurpassed as a seasoning for grilled meats.**

PUNGENT CHEESE HERBS

Use this blend to flavor fresh goat cheese or cream cheese.

2 tablespoons dried basil
1 tablespoon dried parsley
1 tablespoon dried chives
1 tablespoon dried thyme
1 tablespoon dried marjoram
1 teaspoon coarsely cracked black
   pepper

Mix well and store in a jar.

MAKES ABOUT 1/3 CUP

PORK HERBS

3 tablespoons ground coriander
2 tablespoons ground cumin
1 tablespoon ground ginger
2 tablespoons dried sage
1 tablespoon dried savory
1 tablespoon dried thyme

Mix well and store in a jar.

MAKES ABOUT 2/3 CUP

FISH HERBS

3 tablespoons dried dillweed
2 tablespoons dried basil
1 tablespoon dried tarragon
1 tablespoon dried lemon thyme
1 tablespoon dried parsley
1 tablespoon dried chervil
1 tablespoon dried chives

Mix well and store in a jar.

MAKES ABOUT 1/2 CUP

POULTRY HERBS

1 teaspoon dried lovage
1 tablespoon dried marjoram
2 tablespoons dried tarragon
1 tablespoon dried basil
1 tablespoon dried rosemary
1 teaspoon paprika

Mix well and store in a jar.

MAKES ABOUT 1/3 CUP

PICKLING SPICES

Keep this on hand for making pickles.

- 2 tablespoons yellow mustard seeds
- 2 teaspoons whole allspice
- 2 teaspoons black peppercorns
- 2 teaspoons dill seeds
- 2 teaspoons coriander seeds
- 6 bay leaves, crumbled
- 2 small whole red chilies (1½ inch), coarsely broken

Mix well and store in a jar.

MAKES ABOUT 1/3 CUP

POPCORN HERBS

Sprinkle over buttered or unbuttered popcorn in place of salt.

- ¼ cup ground cumin
- 1 tablespoon cayenne or to taste
- 3 tablespoons dried oregano

Mix well and store in a jar.

MAKES ABOUT 1/2 CUP

DESSERT BLEND

This is a quick way to season cookies, cakes, pies, custards, puddings, or fresh fruit.

- 1 tablespoon ground coriander
- 1 tablespoon ground cloves
- 1 tablespoon ground cinnamon
- 1 tablespoon sugar
- 1½ teaspoons aniseed
- 1½ teaspoons fennel seeds
- 1 teaspoon ground ginger

Mix well and store in a jar.

MAKES ABOUT 1/3 CUP

∾ Next time you pop corn, substitute a spicy herbal blend for salt.

RAS EL-HANOUT

This is a very simplified version of the blend available from spice merchants in every Moroccan souk. Each has his own special mixture of as many as 26 different herbs and spices which might include ginger, mace, or exotica such as belladonna berries or cantharis, a bug. Ras el-Hanout is used primarily to flavor Moroccan stews.

3 tablespoons ground cinnamon
1½ tablespoons ground black pepper
1½ tablespoons ground white pepper
2½ teaspoons ground nutmeg
2½ teaspoons ground cloves
2½ teaspoons ground cardamom

Combine the ingredients and store in a jar in a cool, dark place.

MAKES ABOUT 1/2 CUP

MOROCCAN RICE STUFFING

This stuffing, with the peppery sweetness of spices and honey, is an interesting variation on the traditional bread version. Use it to stuff a large capon or a small turkey.

¾ cup butter
½ cup blanched sliced almonds
1½ cups raw white rice
¾ cup raisins
¼ cup ground almonds

1 teaspoon Ras el-Hanout
½ teaspoon ground cinnamon
6 tablespoons sugar
1 large capon or 1 small turkey
(about 10 pounds)
Pinch or 2 of saffron
2 tablespoons honey
Salt to taste

Melt 2 tablespoons of the butter in a small skillet over medium heat. Add the sliced almonds and cook, stirring, until golden brown. Set aside. Cook the rice in boiling water for 10 minutes; drain. Stir the raisins and 4 tablespoons of butter into the rice, place in a colander, and set over boiling water for 10 to 12 minutes. Transfer the rice to a bowl, add the sauteed and ground almonds, Ras el-Hanout, cinnamon, 2 tablespoons butter, and the sugar and mix well. Stuff the capon or turkey.

Blend the saffron with 2 tablespoons of butter and approximately 1 teaspoon of salt and rub the bird all over. Roast the capon or turkey according to your usual method, but about 1 hour before it is done, melt the remaining 2 tablespoons butter and combine it with the honey. Brush this glaze over the bird. If there is any left, reglaze after 30 minutes.

SERVES 6 TO 8

❧ A turkey basted with honey and stuffed with herbed rice evokes the flavors of Morocco.

PEARS WITH HERBED CHEESE AND NASTURTIUM FLOWERS

This combination of pears and cheese is as colorful as it is tasty.

6 to 8 ripe pears
1 pound cream cheese
1 garlic clove
2 tablespoons dry vermouth
3 tablespoons Pungent Cheese Herbs
  (page 36)
6 to 8 nasturtium blossoms

Wash and core the pears. In a small bowl, beat the cream cheese until light and fluffy. Crush the garlic in a press and add to the cheese along with the dry vermouth. Stir until well blended, then mix in the herbs. Stuff the pears and nasturtium blossoms with the cheese mixture. Slice the pears crosswise and arrange on individual plates. Garnish each plate with a stuffed nasturtium blossom.

SERVES 6 TO 8

∾ Crisp pear slices and colorful nasturtium blossoms stuffed with herbed cheese are equally good as an appetizer or dessert.

40

SALT SUBSTITUTES

Although I don't normally use garlic powder, a tiny amount does give added zip to these herbal blends. They can also be used to make a tasty dip by stirring them into sour cream or yogurt.

SAVORY BLEND

2 tablespoons dried dillweed
2 tablespoons dried chives
1 tablespoon dried oregano
2 teaspoons celery seeds
1 teaspoon grated dried lemon peel
½ teaspoon freshly ground pepper

Mix ingredients thoroughly, then pulverize in a blender or use as is, according to taste.

MAKES ABOUT 1/3 CUP

ZESTY BLEND

2 tablespoons dried savory
1 tablespoon dry mustard
1 tablespoon dried chives
2 teaspoons curry powder
1½ teaspoons ground white pepper
1½ teaspoons ground cumin
½ teaspoon garlic powder

Mix ingredients thoroughly and store in a jar in a cool, dark place.

MAKES ABOUT 1/3 CUP

SPICY BLEND

1 tablespoon ground cloves
1 tablespoon cracked black pepper
1 tablespoon crushed coriander seeds
2 tablespoons paprika
1 tablespoon dried winter savory
½ teaspoon garlic powder
½ teaspoon grated dried orange rind

Mix ingredients thoroughly and store in a jar in a cool, dark place.

MAKES ABOUT 1/3 CUP

GARDEN BLEND

3 tablespoons dried parsley
3 tablespoons dried basil
3 tablespoons dried thyme
3 tablespoons dried marjoram
2 tablespoons dried rosemary
2 tablespoons dried chives
2 tablespoons paprika
½ teaspoon garlic powder

Mix the ingredients together, then pulverize them in a blender or use as is, according to taste. Store in a jar in a cool, dark place.

MAKES ABOUT 1 CUP

∾ A simple omelet becomes a gourmet treat with the addition of your favorite herbal blend and sour cream.

JAMS
JELLIES
HONEYS
and SYRUPS

Nowhere is the pungency of herbs as surprising as it is with sweets such as jams and honeys. Many herbal flavors blend exceedingly well with sugar or honey, producing strongly flavored sweeteners that add a delectable nuance to dishes as diverse as lamb stew, fresh fruits, or a rich tea bread. The same counterpoint of sweetness and pungency can also be used to interesting effect in herbal syrups to pour over pancakes, ice cream, or to serve as the basis of a refreshing drink. ❧

43

HERBAL JELLIES

By summer's end, my pantry shelf is lined with jars of herbal jellies ranging from the palest tints of lavender and lemon to the rich amber of rosemary orange marmalade and the deep pink of rhubarb rose jelly. They are so simple to make that every time I have a surplus of a favorite herb or am struck with an idea for a new combination of flavors, I stir up a few jars to add to my collection. Properly sealed, the preservative powers of the sugar keep them fresh for up to six months; for longer storage, process the jellies in a hot-water bath (see page 1).

The most easily made jellies are those based on an herbal infusion. They can feature a single flavor or a combination, be sweet or pungent, suitable for teatime scones or to use as a condiment with meats. Flavoring jellies with a single herb is a good way to get to know the taste of that herb and to give you an idea of which foods it marries with best. Any edible herb can be used, but those with the strongest flavors seem to work best. The addition of a few herbal flowers makes these jellies especially appealing.

Herbs also add their special touch to fruit jellies. Put a small bunch of herbs in with the fruit and sugar while they cook, then discard it and place a fresh sprig in each jar before pouring in the hot jam or jelly. With fruits, the herbs become secondary but add a subtle depth and nuance of flavor, like the soft spiciness lavender gives to strawberry jam. The combinations to try are endless, and so are the pleasures of experimenting and tasting.

☙ **Jars of herb jellies shimmer like jewels in the sun. Lacy doilies and pieces of pretty print fabrics add to their charm.**

BASIC HERB JELLY

This jelly can be made with a variety of herbs and herb flowers. If fresh herbs are not available, substitute one-third the amount of dried herbs. Use vinegar if you are making a jelly to be eaten as a savory with meats or cheese; lemon juice if it is to be eaten as a sweet. Any fruit juice or wine can be used in place of the water for greater variety, and you can combine two or more herbs in one jelly. If you are using flowers that do not seem to be giving up their color in the water, add 2 tablespoons of the vinegar to the water while they are steeping.

The following herbs and/or their flowers are among the many that can be used in this recipe: rosemary, thyme, marjoram, parsley, lemon verbena, mint, any of the scented basils, tarragon, ginger, garlic, chive blossom, lavender, lemon thyme, chamomile, fennel, borage, bee balm, or rose petals (white heel removed).

> 2 cups water or 2½ cups fruit juice
>   or wine
> 1 cup fresh herbs
> 4 cups sugar
> ¼ cup cider vinegar or lemon juice
> 1 to 2 drops food coloring (optional)
> 3 ounces liquid pectin
>   Fresh herb sprigs or ½ cup chopped
>   herbs (optional)

Bring the water or fruit juice to a boil and pour it over the fresh herbs. Cover and steep until the liquid has cooled. Strain, pressing all the liquid and flavor out of the herbs.

In a non-aluminum saucepan combine 2 cups of herbal infusion with the sugar, lemon juice or vinegar, and the food coloring if you are using it. Bring the mixture to a boil over high heat, and as soon as the sugar has dissolved, stir in the pectin. Return to a rolling boil, stirring, and boil for exactly 1 minute. Remove the jelly from the heat and skim off any foam.

If you are using fresh herbs as decoration, place a fresh herb sprig in each jar and hold it in place with a sterilized spoon or chopstick. When the jelly is nearly set, remove the spoon or chopstick and the sprig will stay in place. Stir chopped herbs into the jelly before pouring it into the jars. (If the herbs do not stay suspended, stir the jelly occasionally until it thickens enough to hold.) Process small jars for 5 minutes in a hot-water bath or seal with a thin layer of paraffin.

MAKES 4 TO 5 HALF PINTS

Suggested Combinations

- Apple juice with scented geraniums, sage, thyme, rose petals (with white heels removed), oregano and/or oregano blossoms, mint, or lavender.
- Grapefruit juice with tarragon, mint, calendula petals, marjoram, anise hyssop, or parsley.
- Orange juice with rosemary, thyme, lavender, or basil.
- Pineapple juice with parsley, sage, pineapple sage, coriander, garlic chives, or thyme.
- White wine or white grape juice with lemon geranium, dill and/or dill blossoms, tarragon, pinks, rose petals (with white heels removed), lemon grass, or sweet woodruff.
- Red wine or red grape juice or currant juice with garlic, rosemary, thyme, or savory.

Note: Fresh apple juice contains enough pectin to set without the addition of commercial pectin. If you use it, omit the pectin and boil the jelly until a candy thermometer reaches 220° F. or until a small spoonful sets within a few minutes of being dropped on a plate that has been cooled in the freezer.

∾ **A pink rose adorns this sparkling jar of jelly made from bronze fennel.**

QUICK HERB JELLY

If you are in a hurry or need just one jar of jelly, you can take a shortcut by starting with commercial jelly and adding herbs. The flavor won't be quite as strong, but it will still be delicious.

*1½ pints good-quality apple or
      other jelly*
*1½ tablespoons water or cider vinegar
      Leaves of rose geranium, sprigs of
      rosemary, or other flavorful herbs*

Combine the jelly and water or vinegar in a heavy non-aluminum saucepan. Heat over a low flame, stirring occasionally, until the jelly melts completely. If any foam forms on top, skim it off. Put lightly bruised herbs in a clean jar and pour the hot jelly over them. The hot jelly will wilt the herbs and extract the flavor.

Let the jelly stand until it is partially cool. Remove the wilted herbs with tongs or chopsticks and replace them with a fresh, unbruised leaf or sprig. The jelly should be cool enough so the herb doesn't wilt but still liquid enough to slip the herb in.

MAKES 1/2 PINT

Suggested Combinations

- Orange marmalade with ginger.
- Lemon marmalade with tarragon or thyme.
- Currant jelly with thyme, lavender, or oregano.
- Grape jelly with sage, savory, or marjoram.

HOT PEPPER JELLY

An appealing combination of sweet and hot, this jelly is extremely good with chicken or lamb, or with cream cheese as an hors d'oeuvre.

1 cup minced green bell pepper
*½ cup minced hot red pepper,
      or to taste*
1½ cups cider vinegar
6½ cups sugar
6 ounces liquid pectin

Combine the peppers, vinegar, and sugar in a non-aluminum saucepan and bring to a boil over high heat. Reduce the heat and boil gently for 5 to 7 minutes. Remove from the heat and skim off any foam. Stir in the pectin and pour into sterilized jars. Seal immediately or cool and cover with paraffin.

MAKES 8 HALF PINTS

Note: If the only hot peppers available are green, use a red rather than a green bell pepper.

Glaze grilled baby back ribs, ABOVE, with a sweet-and-hot coating of Hot Pepper Jelly, OPPOSITE, during the last fifteen minutes of cooking.

PEAR GINGER JAM

This spicy jam is equally delicious on toast or with meats.

    2 ounces peeled fresh ginger
2¼ cups sugar
    3 tablespoons white wine
    1 tablespoon rum
    2 cups water
2½ pounds pears, peeled, cored, and
        cut in quarters

Cut the ginger into small pieces and combine in a saucepan with ¼ cup of the sugar and the wine. Cook over medium heat until the sugar has dissolved and the liquid has evaporated. Stir in the rum and set aside.

In a non-aluminum saucepan, cook the water and the remaining 2 cups of sugar together over high heat until the sugar dissolves and the syrup reaches 220° F. on a candy thermometer. Add the pears and the ginger to the syrup, reduce the heat to medium, and cook for 1 hour or until the jam thickens. Skim off any foam and spoon into sterilized jars and seal.

MAKES 3 TO 4 HALF PINTS

STRAWBERRY LAVENDER JAM

The exotic sweetness of lavender produces a soft spiciness when combined with strawberries in this jam.

    1 pound strawberries
    1 pound sugar
    2 dozen lavender stems
     Juice of 2 lemons

Wash, dry, and hull the strawberries. Layer them in a large bowl with the sugar and 1 dozen of the lavender stems and set in a cool place overnight.

Discard the lavender and place the berry mixture in a large non-aluminum saucepan. Tie the remaining lavender stems together and add them to the berries. Add the lemon juice. Cook over medium heat until the mixture comes to a boil, then continue to cook for 20 to 25 minutes. Skim any foam from the top. Discard the lavender and pour the jam into sterilized jars. Seal.

MAKES 3 TO 4 HALF PINTS

LIME GERANIUM JELLY

Try this tart jelly with other herbs such as thyme and rosemary.

1½ cups strained lemon juice
2½ cups strained lime juice
7 cups sugar
1 to 2 drops green food coloring
  (optional)
6 ounces liquid pectin
10 sprigs fresh lime or lemon geranium
  or rose geranium leaves

Combine the juices, sugar, and food coloring if using in a non-aluminum saucepan and bring to a boil over high heat, stirring constantly. Stir the pectin into the juice mixture, return to a rolling boil, stirring, and boil for exactly 1 minute. Remove from the heat and skim off any foam. Place an herb sprig in each jar and pour the jelly over them. Seal.

MAKES 9 TO 10 HALF PINTS

⌒ LEFT: **The ingredients for Strawberry Lavender Jam in a copper jelly kettle.** OVERLEAF: **Savor a variety of herb jellies at a leisurely weekend breakfast.**

RHUBARB ROSE JAM

Rhubarb adds an unexpected tartness to rose jam.

2 pounds rhubarb
3 cups organically grown rose petals
  Juice of 2 lemons
2½ cups sugar for each pint of liquid

Wash the rhubarb and cut it into 1-inch pieces. Wash and dry the rose petals and remove the white heels. Place the fruit and 2 cups of petals in a non-aluminum saucepan, add water to cover, and cook over medium heat until the rhubarb is tender. Stir in the lemon juice.

Strain the fruit through a jelly bag or muslin, without squeezing, until all the liquid has been collected. Measure the liquid and add the sugar and the remaining rose petals. Place the mixture in a non-aluminum saucepan over high heat and bring to a boil. Boil until it has reached 220° F. on a candy thermometer, about 10 minutes. Or test the jam by dropping a small spoonful on a cold plate: it should gel in a few minutes. Seal.

MAKES 5 TO 6 HALF PINTS

ROSEMARY ORANGE MARMALADE

5 sprigs fresh rosemary
2 cups boiling water
4 to 5 oranges
3 cups sugar
3 ounces liquid pectin

Steep 1 sprig of rosemary in the boiling water for 30 minutes; discard the herb sprig. Peel the zest from the oranges, removing as little pith as possible; julienne thinly and place in a saucepan with water to cover. Simmer, covered, about ½ hour or until tender. Drain and reserve.

With a sharp knife free the orange sections from their membranes. Seed the oranges and dice coarsely, then transfer to a non-aluminum saucepan with the rosemary infusion and the sugar and bring to a boil. Boil, stirring frequently, for 35 minutes. Add the pectin and boil for exactly 1 minute. Place a sprig of rosemary in each of 4 half-pint jars and pour the marmalade over them. Seal.

MAKES 4 HALF PINTS

ROSEMARY ORANGE NUT BREAD

This rich and moist tea bread should age, wrapped in aluminum foil, for one day before slicing.

1 cup Rosemary Orange Marmalade
3½ cups all-purpose flour
1 tablespoon baking powder
½ teaspoon salt
2 eggs
1 cup sugar
1 cup milk
2 tablespoons (¼ stick) butter, melted
1 cup chopped walnuts

ORANGE TOPPING
5 tablespoons Orange Rosemary Syrup (page 62)
5 tablespoons confectioner's sugar

Preheat the oven to 350° F.

Place the marmalade in a small saucepan and stir over low heat until it melts. Sift the flour, baking powder, and salt together and set aside in a large bowl. In another bowl, beat the eggs with the sugar; stir in the milk and melted butter and add to the flour mixture, stirring gently just until blended. Mix in the marmalade peel and nuts. Spoon the batter into two greased 9 x 5 x 3-inch loaf pans and bake until done, about 1 hour.

Combine the Orange Rosemary Syrup and sugar. When the bread is done, make several holes in the top of the loaves and pour half the topping mixture over each. Cool in the pan for 15 minutes, then turn onto a rack to finish cooling.

MAKES 2 LOAVES

☙ **Orange Rosemary Syrup glaze keeps this bread moist and adds flavor.**

FLAVORED HONEYS

Long before sugar was widely available, the sweetness of honey was known and enjoyed. A twelve-thousand-year-old Spanish cave painting depicts a Paleolithic man gathering honey in the wild, and ever since then it's been welcome in the kitchen where it's stirred into stews and sauces as well as pastries and ice creams. Except for the occasional marinade, however, most Europeans and Americans tend to reserve honey for desserts and other sweets, but in Middle and Far Eastern countries it is often combined with strong spices and/or salt and used to flavor meats and vegetables, an idea worth borrowing.

Honeys are as varied in their subtleties as wine. They can be smooth to the taste or robust, depending on which flowers the bees have nuzzled in gathering their nectar. Multifloral honeys, which are easier to produce, have a less pronounced flavor than those with the essence of a single plant such as thyme or lavender, but since these richer flavors are more difficult to achieve, they are also more expensive. It's a simple matter, however, to create a good facsimile of herbal honeys in your own kitchen with nothing more than a good basic honey and a few herbs.

∾ Offer herbed honey as an alternative to jams at breakfast.

BASIC HERBED HONEY

Many herbs can be used to flavor honey. Among the most interesting are lavender, thyme, rosemary, mint, roses, bay, linden, cinnamon basil, lemon verbena, rose geranium, or lemon geranium.

> *1 cup honey*
> *1 sprig or several leaves of the fresh herb of your choice*

Heat the honey gently over a low flame. Place the herbs in a clean jar and pour the warm honey over them. Seal and allow to mellow for at least a week before using.

MAKES 1 HALF PINT

SPICY BASIL HONEY

Try this spicy honey on waffles, pancakes, and French toast as well as on vanilla ice cream, yogurt, and fruit.

> *1 cup honey*
> *½ teaspoon ground cinnamon*
> *1 tablespoon brandy*
> *1 sprig basil, preferably cinnamon basil*

Combine the honey, cinnamon, and brandy in a saucepan and heat over low heat. Place the sprig of basil in a sterilized jar and pour the honey over it. Seal and let age for one week before using.

MAKES 1 HALF PINT

LAMB AND ONION TAJINE WITH CINNAMON BASIL HONEY

I translated and adapted the recipe for this delicious dish from a Moroccan cookbook, spurred on by the author's words of description: "You will be applauded by all when you present this dish. The caramelized onions, magnificent and fragrant, must be crushed between the tongue and roof of the mouth, without having need of being chewed."

4½ pounds stewing lamb, cut in
    1½-inch pieces
1 cinnamon stick
1 generous tablespoon ground ginger
    Big pinch of saffron
1¾ cups Basic Herbed Honey made
    with cinnamon basil
2½ pounds small white onions, peeled
    Pinch of salt

Preheat the oven to 400° F.

Combine the lamb, cinnamon, ginger, saffron, and ½ cup of the honey in a large stockpot. Add enough water to cover. Cook until the meat is done and the cooking liquid is reduced by three-quarters, about 1½ hours. If you are lucky enough to have a Moroccan *tajine*, arrange the partially cooked meat and the onions in the bottom and pour the cooking liquid over the meat. Otherwise use a round ovenproof dish 2 inches deep and fashion a cone-shaped cover out of heavy foil, leaving a tiny hole in the top.

Cook the *tajine* for about 1 hour or until the liquid has evaporated and the onions are golden. Warm the remaining honey over a low flame. Remove the *tajine* from the oven and baste the meat and onions with the honey. Return to the oven for 20 minutes to allow the onions to caramelize.

SERVES 10

∾ **Spicy Basil Honey combines with a juicy slice of fresh pineapple and vanilla ice cream for a splendid dessert, LEFT, and Cinnamon Basil Honey glazes a delectable lamb and onion stew, ABOVE.**

HERBAL SYRUPS

Pancakes—and waffles and French toast—seem naked to many people without tawny maple syrup, but pure herb syrups and herb-flavored fruit syrups make for a delicious change of pace. They are equally good poured over fruits and ice cream, stirred into sauces, or, since most are nothing more than a flavored sugar syrup, frozen as a sorbet. Once popular in the United States as the basis for simple refreshing drinks, these syrup-based coolers are still frequently consumed in homes and cafes in many parts of Europe. Although it is possible to find flavored syrups in gourmet shops, it's extremely easy to make these tasty sweeteners at home, and doing so allows you a much wider choice of flavors.

BASIC HERB SYRUP

This syrup can be made with any herb whose flavor pleases you. Drink it straight or pour some over ice and add plain or sparkling water.

3 cups water
1 cup fresh herbs
2 cups sugar

Make an infusion by bringing the water to a boil and pouring it over the herbs. Cover and infuse for several hours. Strain the liquid and combine with the sugar in a non-aluminum saucepan over medium heat. Bring the mixure to a boil; when the sugar dissolves, continue to cook, stirring occasionally, until the syrup thickens, about 10 to 12 minutes. Remove from the heat, cool, and bottle. This syrup will keep in the refrigerator for three months.

MAKES APPROXIMATELY 1 1/2 CUPS

For a nice change of taste, serve pancakes with a selection of herbal syrups.

ORANGE ROSEMARY SYRUP

This syrup is delicious with fruits, in a marinade for chicken or pork, or as the basis of a cooling drink. You can substitute herbs such as mint, lemon balm, or lavender.

3½ cups water
¼ cup chopped fresh rosemary
15 juice oranges
5 cups sugar

In a non-aluminum saucepan, bring the water to a boil. Pour over the rosemary and let steep for 1 hour. Strain.

Remove the zest from 5 of the oranges and set aside, then squeeze the juice into a large bowl. Set a rack over the bowl and arrange the zests on the rack.

Combine the rosemary infusion and the sugar in the saucepan and bring to a boil over high heat, boiling until you have a heavy syrup, about 20 minutes. Pour the boiling syrup over the zests and let it drain into the juice. Return the juice mixture to the saucepan. Bring quickly to a boil, remove from the heat, and return to the bowl to cool. Skim, then bottle and store in the refrigerator.

MAKES 9 CUPS

~ **Festive and unusual, fresh fruits of the season are topped with aromatic herbal syrup.**

STRAWBERRY BALM SYRUP

Delicious with ice cream, waffles, or in a drink. Try making it with lemon verbena or lemon thyme, too.

2 pints strawberries
3 cups sugar, approximately
10 sprigs fresh lemon balm

Wash and hull the strawberries, place in a bowl, and crush with the back of a wooden spoon or a potato masher. Line a medium bowl with cheesecloth, pour the crushed strawberries and their juice into the cloth, then gather up the corners and squeeze until all the juice has been extracted. Weigh the juice, then combine it with an equal amount of sugar and the lemon balm in a non-aluminum saucepan. Bring to a boil and boil for 5 minutes. Remove from the heat, skim any foam from the top, and let cool. Discard the lemon balm before bottling. Store in the refrigerator.

MAKES 1 TO 2 HALF PINTS

Variation

RASPBERRY THYME SYRUP. Substitute 4 half pints of raspberries for the strawberries, and thyme for the lemon balm.

ORANGE SLICES IN MINT SYRUP

Try these orange slices in drinks, or drain them and use as decoration on cakes, puddings, or ice cream. They are also tasty with cold ham or chicken.

2 oranges
1 sprig fresh mint (optional)
2 cups Basic Herb Syrup (page 61)
 made with mint

Wash the oranges thoroughly and slice thinly. Discard the ends and place the remaining slices and the mint, if you are using it, in a wide-mouthed jar with a tight-fitting lid. Cover with the syrup, seal, and macerate for 2 weeks before using. Keep refrigerated after opening.

MAKES 1 PINT

OPPOSITE: **The addition of sparkling water makes Strawberry Balm Syrup a tasty and refreshing drink.** BELOW: **Orange slices in mint syrup can garnish simple desserts or roast poultry.**

PICKLES
and OTHER
DELIGHTS

When gardens are overflowing with vine-ripe cucumbers, crunchy peppers, lush eggplants, and a plethora of herbs, it's time to think about preserving some of the crop for the colder months ahead. Since Roman times pickling has been one of the most popular methods of preserving. ∾ In pickling, the acid in the vinegar acts as a preservative, but covering foods with oil is another time-honored method that works well with many herbs and vegetables. Submerging the food in oil forms a barrier that prevents bacteria in the air from reacting with the food and causing spoilage. ∾

PICKLES

Pickled fruits and vegetables have always been an important part of the cuisines of the Middle and Far East, where they often accompany meals, including breakfast. Once Persian doctors even prescribed them as a treatment for obesity, believing the sour juices neutralized the fat in foods. While they certainly won't promote weight loss, these sharply pungent condiments *are* a delightful companion to pork, duck, sausages, and other fatty foods and a delicious way to add a savory note to any meal.

ABOVE: **Crunchy pickled onions have just a hint of sweetness. For optimum flavor, make your own pickling spices.** OPPOSITE: **A pantry filled with herbed pickles is a cheering sight.**

To many the word "pickle" is synonymous with cucumbers soaked in brine, then treated to a spicy vinegar bath. These "pickles" might be flavored with dill and garlic, scented with tarragon like the French cornichon, or sweetened with sugar—all delicious variations. However, opportunities for pickling exist far beyond cucumbers. Eggs, beans, eggplant, peppers, and onions are among the foods I like to pickle best, but many others can be treated in like manner and enjoyed as part of an antipasto, eaten with hunks of peasant bread and butter for a light lunch, or served with cold meats. But whether sweet or sour, chunky or finely cut, simple or complex, much of the pickles' flavor will come from the herbs and spices you add to the vinegar.

If you plan to keep the pickles for any length of time before using, put them through a hot-water bath (page 1), and once you open the jars, be sure to store them in the refrigerator.

Savory pickled onions and herbed mustard liven up the traditional English ploughman's lunch.

CHRIS'S FAVORITE PICKLED ONIONS

In England, no pub lunch is complete without a few pickled onions.

1 pound small white onions
6 cups water
½ cup salt
2 cups white wine vinegar
1½ tablespoons brown sugar
1 tablespoon Pickling Spices (page 37)
2 small dried chili peppers
2 to 4 bay leaves

Cut the tops and bottoms off the onions but do not peel them. Place them in a deep bowl. In a large pot, bring the water to a boil. Add the salt and stir until it is dissolved. Remove from the heat and let cool slightly. Pour half of this brine over the onions, reserving the rest. Place a plate weighted down with a can on top so the onions will be completely submerged. Let the onions sit in the brine for 24 hours, then drain and peel. Return to the bowl, cover with the remaining brine, and replace the plate. Let them soak for 48 hours, then drain.

In a non-aluminum saucepan, mix the vinegar with the sugar and Pickling Spices and bring to a boil, then boil gently for 5 minutes. Drain the onions and pack them into sterilized jars with a nonmetallic top. Pour the hot vinegar over them, tuck a chili pepper and one or two bay leaves into each jar, and seal. Let stand several weeks before using.

MAKES 2 PINTS

Variation

Use chopped fresh dill, a dill blossom, black peppercorns, and a strip of lemon rind instead of the Pickling Spices, bay, and peppers. Or try tarragon, peppercorns, and red peppers.

DILL PICKLES

1½ pounds small cucumbers
1 large bunch dill
3 garlic cloves
3½ cups white wine vinegar
1½ cups water
3 tablespoons coarse salt
6 black peppercorns
6 white peppercorns

Clean the cucumbers, cut off the ends, and cut into 3-inch pieces. Place the cucumbers in a bowl of ice water, cover with a towel, and let stand 24 hours in the refrigerator. Drain the cucumbers and, using a large needle, puncture each piece in several places. Divide the cucumbers, dill, and garlic equally among three pint jars with tight-fitting lids. In a heavy nonmetallic pan, bring the vinegar, water, salt, and peppercorns to a boil. Pour over the cucumbers and seal immediately. Store in a cool place.

MAKES 3 PINTS

☙ **Dill pickles are an American classic.**

PICKLED EGGS

Another English favorite, pickled eggs are often found on pub bars. The herbs are a French touch.

12 *hard-cooked eggs, peeled*
 2 *bay leaves*
 1 *sprig thyme*
 3 *tablespoons coarsely chopped chives*
 3 *sprigs Italian parsley*
 1 *small chili pepper, fresh or dried*
12 *whole peppercorns*
 3 *cups white wine vinegar*

Layer the eggs and herbs in a jar with a tight fitting lid. Cover with the vinegar and seal. Let stand in a cool, dark place for 1 week before using. The eggs will keep for about two months in the refrigerator. The vinegar may be used in salads and marinades after the eggs are gone.

MAKES 1 DOZEN

Variations

Use only tarragon or a combination of chives, chervil, parsley, and peppercorns. Add a sliced lemon or a sliced onion.

༄ **Pickled eggs are a wonderful addition to a picnic or buffet.**

CUCUMBER PICKLES

A mustardy version of bread and butter pickles.

    4 quarts plus 1 cup water
    1 cup coarse salt
    10 large ripe cucumbers
    4 large onions, sliced
    2 cups cider vinegar
    1 cup rice wine vinegar
1½ cups brown sugar
    2 tablespoons mustard seeds
    1 tablespoon celery seed
    1 tablespoon ground turmeric
    1 large yellow pepper, cubed
    6 sprigs fresh marjoram or tarragon

In a large bowl, make a brine with 4 quarts of water and the salt. Peel the cucumbers, halve lengthwise, and remove the seeds. Cut each half in two, then cut into strips. Place the cucumbers and onion slices in the brine and soak overnight. Drain.

Mix the vinegars, remaining cup of water, sugar, mustard and celery seeds, and turmeric in a non-aluminum saucepan and cook over high heat until the sugar is dissolved, about 5 minutes. Add the drained cucumbers, onion, and yellow pepper and bring to the boiling point but do not boil. Pour into jars with tight-fitting lids. Process in a hot-water bath if you plan to keep the pickles for any time.

MAKES 6 PINTS

GRANDMA POLLEY'S PEPPERHASH

The addition of a few herbs to my grand-mother's recipe makes it even better.

    6 green peppers, finely chopped
    6 red peppers, finely chopped
    1 chili pepper, finely chopped
    7 large onions, finely chopped
    2 cups cider vinegar
    ¾ cup sugar
1½ tablespoons salt
    1 cup fresh thyme sprigs
    6 bay leaves

Place the chopped peppers and onions in a large non-aluminum stock pot and cover with boiling water; let stand for 5 minutes. Drain, cover them with boiling water again, and let stand for 10 minutes. Drain again. Add the vinegar, sugar, salt, half the thyme sprigs tied together, and 2 bay leaves and bring to a boil. Cook, stirring occasionally, until the vegetables are just tender, about 15 minutes. Discard the thyme and bay leaves. Place a fresh thyme sprig and a fresh bay leaf in each jar and ladle the pepperhash into the jars. Seal and process in a hot-water bath.

MAKES 4 TO 5 PINTS

6 cloves garlic, peeled
2 cups water
¼ cup brown sugar
¼ cup nasturtium seeds
3 whole cloves
18 black peppercorns
¼ cup coarse salt
2 juniper berries
2 tablespoons mustard seeds
2 small red chili peppers
5 cups white wine vinegar
6 large sprigs tarragon
6 sprigs chervil

ꤷ **The fiery liquid from Sherry Peppers adds a touch of heat to soups and chowders as well as stews and sauces.**

SHERRY PEPPERS

Sherry infused with hot peppers is an old Bermuda favorite.

1 cup small hot red peppers
2 cups medium dry sherry

Place the peppers in a decorative cruet and cover with the sherry. Let stand 2 weeks before using.

MAKES 1 PINT

VEGETABLE PICKLES

2 cups small cauliflower florets
1½ cups thin green beans
1 cup pearl onions, peeled
1 bunch baby carrots
1 cup asparagus tips
1½ cups seeded and cubed yellow, red, and green peppers
3 small pickling cucumbers, cut in large pieces

Wash the vegetables. If the carrots and beans seem too large to be left whole, cut them into large pieces. Blanch all the vegetables, including the garlic, for 5 minutes in boiling water. Strain and place them in a large pottery or glass container. Bring the vinegar to a boil and pour over the vegetables. Cover and steep for 24 hours. Strain off the vinegar, add the water, sugar, and remaining ingredients except for the tarragon and chervil, and bring to a boil again. Simmer for 2 minutes. Arrange the vegetables attractively in 1 large or several small glass jars with tight-fitting lids, adding the tarragon and chervil. Pour the vinegar over the vegetables, cover, and let stand for 2 weeks before using. Use within 3 weeks or process in a hot-water bath.

MAKES 8 TO 10 HALF PINTS

PICKLED EGGPLANT WITH BASIL

A delightful addition to an antipasto, this can also be used in pasta salads.

12 finger eggplants
¾ cup salt
3 cups white wine vinegar
2 cups water
1 tablespoon sugar
2 teaspoons black peppercorns
1 teaspoon grated fresh ginger
3 garlic cloves, peeled
24 large basil leaves
4 sprigs parsley
4 sprigs marjoram or oregano

Wash and dry the eggplants, then cut into quarters. Sprinkle ½ cup salt over the cut sides and set aside to drain for 30 minutes. Wipe the pieces of eggplant dry and reserve. In a non-aluminum saucepan, bring the vinegar, water, sugar, ¼ cup salt, peppercorns, ginger, and garlic to a boil. Reduce the heat to medium, add the eggplant, and simmer for 5 minutes. Remove the garlic and divide the eggplant among 4 sterilized pint jars with tight-fitting lids. Add 6 basil leaves and a sprig of parsley and marjoram or oregano to each jar. Process in a hot-water bath for 15 minutes. Let stand at least 2 weeks before using.

MAKES 4 PINTS

∾ **Pickled eggplant adds interest to an antipasto platter.**

PRESERVING IN OIL

Foods preserved in oil have a gentler flavor than those pickled in vinegar and there is the bonus of a supply of deliciously flavored oil to be used for cooking and salads once the food has been consumed. And many foods that can be marinated in oil benefit from the addition of pungent herbs and spices that enhance their natural flavors. Sun-dried tomatoes are delicious when flavored with spicy basil leaves, although rosemary works just as well. Certain herbs such as basil and tarragon retain more flavor when preserved in oil than with other methods, and are ready to be added to soups, stews, and sauces whenever you need them, and herb pastes are convenient for dozens of uses.

Use these recipes as a guide for devising your own favorite combinations of herbs and vegetables. Foods preserved by this method should last up to six months in a cool place or in the refrigerator. If you plan to keep them longer, process them in a hot-water bath.

➤ ABOVE: **A colorful assortment of peppers in oil adds zest to salads, sandwiches, and antipastos.** OPPOSITE: **Sautéed mushrooms, ready to be packed in jars.**

PEPPERS IN OIL

You can use mild, hot, or a variety of peppers in this recipe.

> 2 pounds assorted peppers
>   Coarse salt
> 6 garlic cloves
> 6 sprigs fresh mint
> 12 peppercorns
> 1 tablespoon salt
>   Olive oil to cover

Cut the peppers in half lengthwise and remove the ribs and seeds. (If you are using hot peppers, wear gloves so you do not burn your hands.) Dry the peppers on a clean towel, then cut them in strips. Place them in a large bowl, sprinkle with coarse salt, and let drain overnight. Dry the peppers again.

Add the garlic, mint, peppercorns, and salt. Pack into hot sterilized jars, cover completely with oil, and seal immediately. Keep in a cool place or process in a hot-water bath for 15 minutes.

MAKES 3 TO 4 HALF PINTS

SUN-DRIED TOMATOES

These dried tomatoes have such a concentrated tomato taste, just a few will add immeasurable flavor to salads, pasta sauces, pizzas, or any other dish where a touch of tomato is desired. Although they can actually be dried in the sun (bring them in at night so the dew doesn't dampen them), it is more convenient for most of us to dry them in the oven or a dehydrator set at 200° F.

➦ **Earthy Sun-Dried Tomatoes.**

6 *pounds plum tomatoes*
  Salt
2 *to 3 sprigs fresh basil*
2 *to 3 garlic cloves (optional)*
  Olive oil to cover

Preheat the oven to 200° F.

Cut the tomatoes in half lengthwise, leaving them attached at the bottom end, and open them like a book. Line a baking sheet with foil and set a rack on top. Place the tomatoes on the rack, cut side up, with enough space around them to allow air to circulate. Sprinkle the cut side lightly with salt. Put the tomatoes in the oven, leaving the door slightly ajar so moisture can escape. The tomatoes are done when they are slightly shriveled, deep red, and dry but not crisp, about 6 hours. Do not allow them to burn.

When the tomatoes are done, remove them from the oven, cool, and pack into sterilized jars. Add 1 basil sprig and, if desired, 1 clove of garlic to each jar. Pour in enough olive oil to cover the tomatoes and herbs completely, seal, and store in the refrigerator.

MAKES 2 TO 3 PINTS

MUSHROOMS IN OIL

These delicious mushrooms can be used in omelets, in sauces, or just quickly sautéed to accompany meats.

1 pound cepes
2 cups white wine vinegar
1 garlic clove, minced
2 cups olive oil
2 bay leaves
2 sprigs fresh thyme
6 peppercorns

Wipe the mushrooms clean and peel if necessary. Cut the woody end from the stem, separate the stem from the cap, and cut both into thick slices. Bring the wine to a boil in a non-aluminum saucepan over a high heat. Cook the mushroom slices in the boiling liquid for 2 minutes, then refresh under cold running water. Dry the mushrooms completely. Warm the oil in a sauté pan over low heat; add the garlic and cook for about 5 minutes without browning. Layer the mushrooms into sterilized jars with the herbs and pour the warm garlic oil over them, making sure they are completely covered. Seal. These mushrooms can be stored safely in the refrigerator for 2 to 3 months.

MAKES 4 HALF PINTS

HERB PASTES

In Italy, basil leaves are frequently preserved by packing them in a jar and covering them with olive oil. Although this is quite satisfactory, even handier is an herbal paste prepared by pureeing the herbs in oil which can be stored in the freezer or in the refrigerator. When you need a touch of herbal flavoring for a stew, soup, or sauce, it's a simple matter to spoon out the amount you need.

Among the herbs that preserve most successfully this way are parsley, coriander, basil, mint, sorrel, and tarragon, but you can experiment with others.

2 cups fresh herb leaves
½ cup olive oil
Additional oil to float on top
if needed

Combine the herb leaves and the half cup of olive oil in a food processor or blender and puree until very finely minced. Pack in sterilized jars and store in the freezer or the refrigerator. If you opt for the refrigerator, be sure the paste in the jar is always covered with a thin layer of oil to prevent the formation of mold.

MAKES ABOUT 3/4 CUP

Preserve mushrooms in oil when they're in season, then enjoy their woodsy flavor later.

GOAT CHEESE AND SUN-DRIED TOMATO TORTE

The heady flavors of tomatoes, basil, and goat cheese combine perfectly in this appealing hors d'oeuvre.

   8 ounces cream cheese, softened
   12 ounces Montrachet goat cheese
   ½ pound (2 sticks) butter, softened
   1 cup Basil Pesto (page 107)
   1 cup drained, minced Sun-Dried
      Tomatoes (page 78)

Place the cheeses and butter in a bowl and beat together until they are well blended and fluffy. Line an 8-inch cake pan with dampened cheesecloth, leaving enough extra to fold over the top. Layer one third of the cheese mixture in the bottom and spread half of the pesto over it. Repeat. Spread the remaining cheese on top and cover with the minced tomatoes. Place a piece of plastic wrap over the top and fold the cheesecloth over it. Set the torte in the refrigerator for at least an hour to firm up. When ready to serve, fold the cheesecloth back, turn the torte onto a plate, and remove the cheesecloth. Invert the torte onto a serving plate and remove the plastic wrap. Serve with assorted crackers.

SERVES 15 TO 20

∾ **This attractive torte can be frozen for impromptu entertaining.**

OLIVES

Around the Mediterranean, where they originated, olives are a staple in every kitchen and often find their way into the main dish. Whether picked when they are green or allowed to ripen to black, these Mediterranean olives are cured in a salt brine, then bathed in olive oil that generally

contains a few herbs and spices. These delicious morsels bear little resemblance to the olives you find on supermarket shelves. In fact, I didn't particularly like olives until I tasted some that had been given added zest with fennel seed and orange rind. Although olives marinated in oil are available in gourmet stores, it's quite easy and much less expensive to transform good-quality unpitted black or green canned olives or commercially packaged air-cured olives into enticing treats with some good oil and a few flavorful sprigs from the herb garden. Avoid the bright green salted and stuffed varieties.

A few specific suggestions on how to transform olives follow, but there is no rule as to which herbs and spices go with what—just be sure to cover the olives with the oil. Don't worry if this seems to take quite a bit of oil. As you use the olives, add new ones to the oil in the jar, or filter the oil and add it to salads, marinades and the like.

The basic method for making herbed olives is simple. After draining and rinsing the olives, mix them with the herbs and/or spices and place them in a jar with a tight-fitting lid. Pour the oil over them and allow them to marinate for at least 2 days before using. (If you've used garlic, remove it after a few days so its strong flavor doesn't overwhelm the other ingredients.) The olives will keep in the refrigerator for 6 months. Bring to room temperature before serving.

∾ ABOVE: **Olives infused with zesty lemon and fennel seeds for cocktail time. OPPOSITE: Herb-marinated olives are instant party fare.**

CORIANDER OLIVES

- 1 pound black olives
- 1 small fresh hot pepper, seeded and cut in strips
- 1/2 cup coarsely chopped fresh corianaer
- 1 teaspoon black peppercorns
  Olive oil to cover

ZESTY OLIVES

- 1 pound green olives
- 3 garlic cloves, peeled
- 1 1/2 teaspoons dried thyme
- 1 1/2 teaspoons dried oregano
- 1 bay leaf, crushed
- 2 slices lemon
- 1 teaspoon allspice
  Olive oil to cover

LEMON FENNEL OLIVES

- 1 pound green olives
- 4 garlic cloves
- 1 tablespoon fennel seeds
  Zest and juice of 1 lemon
  Olive oil to cover

~ An assortment of herbed olives, LEFT TO RIGHT: **Lemon Fennel Olives, Zesty Olives, Coriander Olives, and Franklin Adams's Kalamata Olives.**

FRANKLIN ADAMS'S KALAMATA OLIVES

1 pound Kalamata or other
  black olives
1 teaspoon orange zest
6 hot peppers, dried or fresh
  Few sprigs fresh rosemary
  Few sprigs fresh thyme
  Few springs fresh Greek oregano
  Olive oil to cover

TIPSY OLIVES

1 pound green olives
¼ cup sherry
2 tablespoons mustard seeds
1 teaspoon dried red pepper flakes
  Olive oil to cover

ORANGE CARDAMOM OLIVES

1 pound black olives
  Zest of 2 oranges, cut in strips
2 teaspoons cardamom seeds, lightly
  crushed
1 teaspoon white peppercorns
  Olive oil to cover

THYME AND GARLIC OLIVES

¾ pound black olives
3 garlic cloves, peeled and minced
1 to 2 tablespoons fresh thyme leaves
   or 1 to 2 teaspoons dried
1 teaspoon white peppercorns
   Olive oil to cover

FOCACCIA WITH THYME AND GARLIC OLIVES

I like to use whole unpitted olives for this *focaccia,* but if you would like to make it easier for your guests to eat, halve and pit the olives before sprinkling them over the dough.

1 package dry yeast
1½ cups warm water (110° F.)
4 cups unbleached flour or bread flour
2 teaspoons salt
¼ cup oil from Thyme and Garlic
   Olives and oil for the top
1 tablespoon dried thyme or
   3 tablespoons fresh
1 cup Thyme and Garlic Olives,
   drained

Dissolve the yeast in ¼ cup warm water, letting it stand until it becomes milky and bubbly. Place the flour and the salt in a large bowl and make an indentation in the center. Pour in the yeast mixture, the

remaining water, and the ¼ cup of the olive oil. Mix well. Turn the dough out onto a floured board and knead for 15 minutes or until it is soft and silky, adding more flour if necessary.

Shape the dough into a ball, dust lightly with flour, place in a lightly oiled bowl, and cover with a damp towel. Allow the dough to rise in a warm, draft-free place until doubled in bulk, about 35 to 40 minutes

Preheat the oven to 400° F.

Punch the dough down and place on a greased baking sheet. Let it rest a few minutes, then stretch it with your fingers to completely cover the bottom. Cover with a damp towel and let rest 20 to 30 minutes. With the fingertips, make a uniform pattern of indentations in the dough. Brush generously with oil and sprinkle with thyme. Place olives in the indentations and bake about 30 to 35 minutes.

MAKES 1 LARGE LOAF

❧ **Pungent thyme imparts its flavor to both the dough and olive topping of this delicious** *focaccia.*

CHUTNEYS MUSTARDS and SAUCES

The tantalizing flavor of condiments elevates the plainest slice of meat, cheese, or sandwich to the status of culinary treat. Sometimes hot, always tangy, and occasionally touched with sweetness, chutneys, mustards, and herbal sauces are easy ways to enhance simple dishes, but they are also an interesting

counterpoint to more complex tastes. In condiments herbs can star, as in mint sauce, horseradish sauce, or pesto, or simply provide a bit of extra zip. And mustard, itself an herb, becomes a more sophisticated and appetizing blend when flavored with other herbs. ❧

CHUTNEYS

Almost any fruit or vegetable can be turned into the delightful sweet-and-sour condiment known as chutney. Although most often associated with food from India, chutneys are actually quite British, an invention of the colonials who governed India and named their concoction after the Hindustani word for strong spices, *chatni*. The pieces of fruit or vegetable can be cut large or small, or even pureed, but they are always cooked with vinegar, sugar, and a selection of herbs and spices until the liquid becomes syrupy and the chutney resembles jam. An indispensable accompaniment to curries, they are also splendid with a variety of simply broiled or sliced cold meats, poultry, fish, or sharp cheddar cheese.

HOT TOMATO CHUTNEY

A delicious accompaniment to cold meats and chicken.

3 pounds (about 4 to 5) ripe tomatoes, seeded and coarsely chopped
1 cup brown sugar
1 cup cider vinegar
1 large red pepper, chopped
1 large onion, coarsely chopped
2 garlic cloves, minced
3 tablespoons peeled and minced fresh ginger
½ cup raisins
2 jalapeño peppers, seeded and chopped
1 teaspoon cumin seeds
1 teaspoon mustard seeds
2 teaspoons salt
¼ cup chopped cilantro

Place all the ingredients except the cilantro in a large non-aluminum saucepan and cook over medium heat, stirring, until the sugar is dissolved. Continue to cook, stirring occasionally, until the mixture thickens, about 30 minutes. Stir in the cilantro for the last few minutes of cooking. Pack in sterilized jars and seal. Freeze or process in a hot-water bath for 15 minutes.

MAKES 3 TO 4 PINTS

∾ **Hot Tomato Chutney complements hot and cold meats.**

NANCY'S BANANA CHUTNEY

A friend once gave me a jar of this slightly sweet chutney and I've been making it ever since.

2 cups coarsely chopped onion
1 pound dates, chopped
6 ripe bananas
3 cups sugar
2 cups cider vinegar
1 cup golden raisins
½ to ¾ cup crystallized ginger
1 teaspoon curry powder
1 teaspoon salt

Combine all the ingredients in a heavy non-aluminum saucepan. Bring to a boil over medium heat, then simmer until thick, stirring occasionally, about 30 minutes. Spoon into half-pint jars, seal, and store in the refrigerator.

MAKES 8 HALF PINTS

↩ Ruby red Cranberry Sage Chutney.

CRANBERRY SAGE CHUTNEY

This chutney is wonderful with a holiday turkey and the turkey sandwiches that follow. It would also make a great Christmas present for friends.

6 cups cranberries
1½ cups sugar
1 orange, unpeeled, chopped, and seeded
1 cup orange juice
1 small onion, finely chopped
¼ cup raisins
¼ cup slivered almonds
12 dried dates, chopped
¼ cup chopped crystallized ginger
½ cup cider vinegar
1 teaspoon salt
1 teaspoon dry mustard
3 tablespoons chopped fresh sage

Place all the ingredients except 2 tablespoons of the sage in a non-aluminum pan and cook over medium low heat, stirring, until the sugar dissolves. Increase the heat and boil until the berries pop and the mixture thickens slightly, about 5 to 10 minutes. Stir in remaining tablespoons of sage. Ladle into sterilized jars, wipe the rims clean, and seal tightly. This chutney can be refrigerated for up to 6 months. To store for up to one year, process in a hot-water bath (page 1) for 15 minutes. Store in a cool, dark place.

MAKES 8 HALF PINTS

MINT CHUTNEY

This is interesting served with lamb as an alternative to the usual mint jelly, and is also good with pears or apples and cheese as a savory.

1½ cups brown sugar
 1 tablespoon mustard seeds
1½ cups cider vinegar
 3 cups finely chopped apple mint or other mint
 1 cup finely chopped cilantro or parsley
 3 cups peeled and finely chopped apples
 2 medium yellow onions, finely chopped
 ½ cup seedless raisins
 ½ cup chopped walnuts
 1 teaspoon salt

Place the sugar, mustard seed, and vinegar in a non-aluminum pan over low heat and cook, stirring, until the sugar has dissolved. Add the remaining ingredients and bring to a boil. Reduce heat and simmer for 5 to 10 minutes or until the chutney has thickened Pour into sterilized jars and seal. Store in the refrigerator for up to 2 months or process in a hot-water bath for 15 minutes for longer storage.

MAKES 3 PINTS

PINEAPPLE PARSLEY CHUTNEY

Try this with cold fish, pork, or ham.

 4 cups diced fresh pineapple
 ½ cup brown sugar
 1 cup cider vinegar
 1 tablespoon mustard seeds
 1 teaspoon coriander seeds
 1 small garlic clove, minced
 1 red pepper, chopped
 1 onion, coarsely chopped
 1 jalapeño pepper, chopped
 ½ cup raisins
 ¼ cup crystallized ginger
 1 lime, seeded and thinly sliced
 ½ cup chopped parsley

Place all the ingredients except the parsley into a large non-aluminum saucepan. Cook over medium heat, stirring, until the sugar dissolves, then continue to cook, stirring occasionally, until the mixture thickens, about 30 minutes. Add the parsley during the last few minutes of cooking. Ladle into jars and seal. Freeze, or process for 15 minutes in a hot-water bath.

MAKE 3 PINTS

∾ LEFT: **Pineapple Parsley Chutney contrasts the sweetness of fruit with the fiery flavors of jalapeño, ginger, and mustard seeds. OVERLEAF: Mint Chutney is delicious with cheese.**

APRICOT LEMON BASIL CHUTNEY

If lemon basil is unavailable, substitute regular or cinnamon basil, lemon balm, or marjoram.

1 pound dried apricots
1½ cups brown sugar
1½ cups cider vinegar
1 medium onion, coarsely chopped
½ cup golden raisins
½ cup sliced blanched almonds
2 garlic cloves, finely chopped
2 tablespoons peeled and minced fresh ginger
1 tablespoon salt
1 teaspoon coriander seeds, lightly crushed
½ teaspoon cayenne pepper
¼ cup chopped lemon basil

Place all ingredients except the basil in a large, heavy non-aluminum saucepan and cook over low heat, stirring, until the sugar dissolves. Increase the heat and bring to a boil, then reduce the heat and simmer, stirring occasionally, until the mixture thickens, about 45 minutes to 1 hour. Stir in the chopped basil, place in sterilized jars, and cover tightly. Refrigerate, freeze, or process in a hot-water bath for 15 minutes.

MAKES 5 TO 6 HALF PINTS

～ **Although not strictly authentic, Ruby's Chicken Curry is delicious.**

RUBY'S CHICKEN CURRY

Serve with rice and dishes of coconut, peanuts, almonds, bacon, chopped egg, and more chutney.

¼ cup (½ stick) butter
2 large yellow onions, chopped
4 tablespoons curry powder
1 cup chicken broth
4 cups cubed cooked chicken
2 cups fresh pineapple cut in large cubes
2 just-ripe bananas, sliced
1 large green apple, diced
1 cup coarsely shredded fresh coconut
½ cup coarsely chopped almonds
½ cup Apricot Lemon Basil Chutney
1 cucumber, coarsely chopped
Juice of 1 lemon
1 cup heavy cream

Melt the butter in a large skillet over medium heat. Add the onion and sauté until it is soft but not brown, about 5 to 7 minutes. Stir in the curry powder and cook, stirring, for 2 minutes, then stir in the broth. Add all the remaining ingredients except the cream. Cover and cook over a low flame for about 2 minutes or until the fruits are tender and the flavors have had time to blend. Just before serving, stir in the cream.

SERVES 6

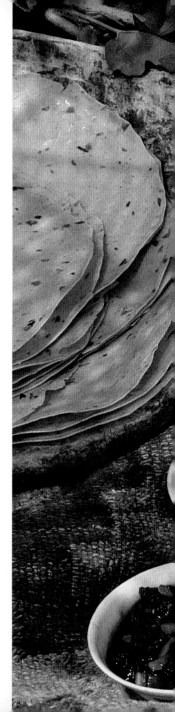

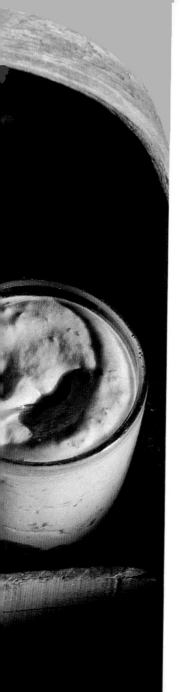

MUSTARDS

The pungent flavor of mustard seed has been enhancing food since early Greek and Roman gourmets pounded the seeds with a little new wine into a rather primitive condiment. Later the Romans carried mustard north to England, and no English kitchen has been without this spicy condiment since. It was an Englishman, Mr. Coleman, who perfected the art of grinding mustard into a fine powder, but the more adventuresome Italians flavored their mustards with lemon and orange peel and the French combined the seed with white wine and spices to perfect the classic Dijon blend.

Today mustard is a staple in every kitchen, and in mine you're liable to find a selection ready to add noncaloric zest to everything except desserts. Most days a fine Dijon or English mustard will suffice, but I enjoy adding other herbs and spices to the basics for an interesting change of pace. Sometimes I even tailor the mustard flavor for specific foods: dill or fennel seed, for example, when fish is on the menu; or tarragon to accompany chicken or seafood.

The easiest way of making flavored mustards is to start with a prepared Dijon mustard and add the herbs of your choice, but you can create an even wider range of tastes if you use powdered mustard and mustard seed. The sharpness of the mustard is greatly affected by the liquid used: vinegar produces an English-style mustard; champagne or white wine, a Dijon type; flat beer, the fiery Chinese version; and plain water, the hottest (and least interesting) of all. Whichever liquid you use, however, start by allowing the mustard to steep for 15 minutes to develop its flavor to the fullest and eliminate any bitterness.

⌒ Herbal mustards are simple to make by combining your favorite herbs with prepared Dijon mustard.

I pack my mustards in small jars with tight-fitting lids and store them in a cool, dark place or the refrigerator. This way I have a variety to choose from to spice up my cooking or make cold meats especially tasty, as well as a reserve for giving to friends.

~ **Coat a baked ham with a blend of herbed mustard and apricot jam.**

QUICK HERBED MUSTARD

1½ cups Dijon mustard
¼ cup or to taste chopped fresh basil, mint, thyme, chives, marjoram, rosemary, or other herbs of your choice
1½ tablespoons dry white wine

Mix all the ingredients together well, place in a sterilized jar with a tight-fitting lid, and store in a cool, dark place for up to 3 months.

MAKES 1 1/2 CUPS

Variation

MUSTARD PROVENCAL: Replace the fresh herb with 1 heaping tablespoon of Herbes de Provence (page 36) soaked in the wine for a few minutes to soften them. Or try the same amount of Fines Herbes (page 35). Either would be good with beef.

CITRUS MUSTARD

Delicious with cold ham, chicken, veal, or pork.

2 cups Dijon mustard
1 tablespoon lemon juice
1 tablespoon orange juice
1 teaspoon honey
1 tablespoon chopped lemon thyme
2 teaspoons each grated lemon and orange rind

Whisk all the ingredients together.

MAKES 2 1/4 CUPS

Variations

ORANGE MUSTARD: Use an extra tablespoon of orange juice in place of the lemon juice, rosemary or orange mint instead of lemon thyme, and add 1 teaspoon ground cumin.

LIME MUSTARD: Use lime juice instead of orange juice, and lime rind instead of orange rind.

TARRAGON MUSTARD

Excellent with cold fish and seafood, chicken, beef, veal, or eggs.

1 cup dry mustard
2 tablespoons mustard seeds
½ cup brown sugar
⅓ cup tarragon vinegar
½ teaspoon salt
¼ cup olive oil
¼ cup chopped fresh tarragon or 1½ tablespoons dried

Combine the dry mustard, mustard seeds, sugar, vinegar, and salt in a blender or processor and mix until smooth. Add the olive oil in a slow stream while continuing to blend. The mustard should have the consistency of mayonnaise. Stir in the tarragon and pack into sterilized, tightly sealed jars. Store in a cool, dark place or in the refrigerator.

MAKES 2 CUPS

LEMON DILL MUSTARD

Eat this with cold fish and seafood.

2 cups Dijon mustard
¼ cup chopped fresh parsley
¼ cup chopped fresh dill
1 tablespoon lemon juice
1 tablespoon lemon rind

Mix all ingredients together well.

MAKES 2 1/2 CUPS

Variations

Substitute fennel leaves for the dill or use 1 tablespoon of dill or fennel seeds in place of the fresh herb, or use cilantro, thyme, lemon balm, sage, or savory in place of the dill.

ABOVE: **Cold shrimp get a dollop of sour cream seasoned with Lemon Dill Mustard.** LEFT: **A dish of Tarragon Mustard.**

HORSERADISH MUSTARD

Try this peppery mustard with cold beef, ham, cheese, or cold seafood.

> 3 tablespoons mustard seeds
> 1 cup dry mustard
> ½ cup sugar
> ½ cup white wine vinegar
> ¼ cup olive oil
> ½ teaspoon lemon juice
> ¼ cup Horseradish Sauce (page 105)

Soak the mustard seeds in one cup of hot water for 1 hour; drain and place in a food processor with the remaining ingredients. Process for 1 minute, then scrape down the sides and process for an additional 30 seconds. Pack into sterilized jars and store in the refrigerator.

MAKES ABOUT 1 1/2 CUPS

❧ French bread, homemade pepperhash, and herbed mustard make a hot dog gourmet fare.

SWEET TOMATO MUSTARD TART

A flavorful dish for lunch or a light supper. For a more Italian flavor, substitute mozzarella cheese for the Gruyère.

> 3 tablespoons Quick Herbed Mustard
>   (page 100) made with basil
> 1 10-inch pâté brisé tart shell,
>   uncooked
> ½ pound Gruyère cheese, thinly sliced
> 6 ripe tomatoes, sliced about
>   ¼ inch thick
> 3 tablespoons brown sugar
>   Salt and pepper to taste
>   Fresh basil for garnish

Preheat the oven to 425° F.

Bake the crust for 10 minutes, remove from the oven, and cool slightly.

Spread the mustard over the bottom of the cooled crust. Top with the cheese, then the tomatoes. Sprinkle the brown sugar over the tomatoes and season to taste. Bake until the crust is golden brown, the cheese is melted, and the tomatoes are tender, about 15 to 20 minutes. Garnish with fresh basil.

SERVES 6

❧ A juicy Sweet Tomato Mustard Tart, enhanced with Basil Mustard and brown sugar, is the perfect dish for a luncheon or a light supper.

HERBAL SAUCES

Sauces can be hot or cold, used in cooking or added at serving time, and are often the element that sets a dish apart. Many, such as traditional mint sauce, are distinguished by the flavorful herbs for which they are named. Horseradish and mustard sauces are two other time-honored favorites. More recently pesto—which has become almost synonymous with basil, although it can be made with a variety of other herbs—has become most popular of all. Like many of the other foods in this book, these basic sauces can easily be altered to suit your menu simply by substituting a more appropriate herb.

⌒ **The definitive flavor of Anise Hyssop Sauce, ABOVE, enlivens simple grilled tuna, RIGHT.**

MINT SAUCE

This sauce, traditionally served with lamb, can also be used with cold seafood or mixed with mayonnaise or oil to make a dressing for fruit or potato salad.

1 cup cider vinegar
3 tablespoons sugar
½ cup minced fresh mint leaves

Combine the vinegar and sugar in a saucepan and cook over moderately low heat, stirring, until the sugar is dissolved. Remove from the heat, cool slightly, then add the mint and infuse for at least 30 minutes. Strain if desired. The sauce will keep in the refrigerator for several weeks.

MAKES ABOUT 1 CUP

Variations

ANISE HYSSOP SAUCE: Substitute an equal amount of anise hyssop for the mint and serve with tuna and other firm fish, in fish or potato salads, or with pork.

LEMON VERBENA SAUCE: Substitute an equal amount of lemon verbena for the mint and reduce the sugar to 2 tablespoons. Complements fruits, chicken salad, fish, and vegetables.

TARRAGON SAUCE: Substitute an equal amount of tarragon for the mint. Delicious with chicken, beef, eggs, or fish.

HORSERADISH SAUCE

To use, stir in some sour cream or whipped cream, some lingonberry or cranberry jelly or applesauce, or a combination of cream and jelly. Serve with cold meats, boiled beef, or pork.

½ cup grated horseradish root
3 tablespoons white vinegar
1 teaspoon salt
Dash of cayenne

Mix all ingredients together and store in a covered jar in the refrigerator.

MAKES ABOUT 1/2 CUP

Variation

GINGER SAUCE: Substitute grated ginger root for the horseradish, and blend with orange marmalade or cherry jam. Serve with roast duck, pork, or chicken.

↜ Horseradish Sauce is an essential part of a New England boiled dinner.

BASIL PESTO

Although basil is the herb most commonly found in pesto, other herbs can be used with equal success. In Italy, where this delectable sauce originated, parsley is often substituted when basil is unavailable. And although they are known primarily as pasta sauces, pestos can be added to chicken or vegetable soups; spread on toasted peasant bread and covered with sliced tomatoes; thinned with mayonnaise or sour cream to use as a sandwich spread or on seafood or pasta salads, baked potatoes, or as a dip for crudités; or spread on the bottom crust of a tomato quiche, tart, or pizza.

> 2 cups fresh basil leaves
> ½ cup parsley leaves
> ½ cup olive oil
> 3 tablespoons pine nuts
> 2 garlic cloves, peeled
> ¾ cup freshly grated Parmesan cheese
> 2 tablespoons soft butter
> Salt to taste

Puree the basil, parsley, olive oil, nuts, and garlic in a food processor or blender. Mix the cheese and butter in by hand (see Note). Season to taste. If the pesto is too thick, just before serving add a spoonful or two of pasta cooking water or other liquid.

MAKES ABOUT 1 1/2 CUPS

Note: If you are not going to use the pesto immediately, pour a thin layer of oil on top of the pesto and store it in the refrigerator. If you prefer to freeze it, add the cheese and butter after thawing.

Variations

MINT PESTO: Substitute mint for the basil and parsley, walnuts for the pine nuts, and use it to coat a leg of lamb, lamb chops, or chicken, or on chicken or lamb sandwiches.

CILANTRO PESTO: Substitute cilantro for the basil and add a little lemon or lime juice. Use with chicken, fish, lamb, or in seafood pasta salads.

TARRAGON PESTO: Substitute tarragon for the basil and use walnuts instead of pine nuts. Good with chicken, fish, and vegetable salads.

ROSEMARY PESTO: Substitute 1 cup of rosemary for the basil. Increase the parsley to 2 cups. Use with beef, chicken, lamb, or potatoes.

◝ Tarragon Pesto is particularly good with chicken and fish, either as a precooking seasoning or in a sauce for the finished dish.

VEGETABLE STEW WITH PESTO

This hearty side dish is equally good in summer or winter. If you can't find ripe tomatoes, substitute 2 cups of drained whole canned tomatoes, chopped.

- 1 large eggplant, cubed
- 1 tablespoon coarse salt
- 1 green pepper
- 1 red pepper
- ¼ cup olive oil
- 2 onions, peeled and sliced
- 3 garlic cloves, crushed
- 6 tomatoes, peeled, seeded, and finely chopped
- 4 small zucchini, cut in 2-inch pieces
- ½ cup chicken broth
- 2 tablespoons Basil Pesto (page 107)
  Salt and pepper to taste
- 4 potatoes, peeled and cubed
- 2 tablespoons Parmesan cheese
- 2 tablespoons chopped fresh basil
- 2 tablespoons chopped fresh parsley

Place the eggplant in a colander, sprinkle with coarse salt, and set aside to drain for 1 hour. Wipe dry. Char the skins of the peppers under the broiler, then place them in a brown paper bag for 5 minutes. Peel, seed, and cut the peppers in strips, holding them over a small bowl to catch any juices.

Heat the olive oil in a large pot over a medium flame, add the onions, and cook for about 5 minutes or until the onions start becoming transparent. Add the eggplant and garlic and cook an additional 5 minutes, or until the eggplant begins to brown. Add the tomatoes, zucchini, any juices from the peppers, and the chicken broth combined with the pesto to the eggplant mixture. Season with salt and pepper, then cook, covered, over low heat for 20 minutes. Stir the potatoes into the stew and cook, covered, an additional 20 minutes or until the potatoes are done. Combine the cheese and chopped herbs and sprinkle on top of the stew before serving.

SERVES 8 TO 10

∾ LEFT: **Tiny boiled new potatoes spread with Rosemary Pesto.**
RIGHT: **Basil Pesto enriches a hearty vegetable stew.**

~ HERBAL LIBATIONS

Many famous liqueurs get their distinctive tastes from herbs steeped in alcohol, so why not use the herbs from your garden to make your own delicious after-dinner drinks? Anise and mint are favorite liqueur flavorings, while herbal blends produce the subtle flavors of Chartreuse and Benedictine. Steeping wine with fruit and herbs produces a lively aperitif. ❧ *And if you want something gentler, a cup of herbal tea can be incredibly soothing hot or pleasantly refreshing iced. Depending on the herbs used, they can also comfort a cold, lull you to sleep, or give your energy a boost.* ❧

HERBAL LIQUEURS

These delicious libations had their origins in the Middle Ages, when monks and alchemists, in search of a cure for man's many ills, used alcohol to extract the oils from herbs and spices. Although they never found a panacea, they did discover many wonderful potions treasured for their flavor alone. When the spice trade brought new herbs from the East in the 1600s, more complex blends were developed and these tasty drinks with their closely guarded recipes soon became a source of income for many monasteries. Carthusian monks, isolated in the massif of the Grand Chartreuse in France, blended 130 different herbs and spices to create Chartreuse, which became so famous that its name is now synonymous with its distinctive yellow-green hue. Twenty-seven herbs, including angelica, tea, juniper berries, and vanilla, were used by the Benedictines in distilling their equally well known liqueur.

Fruit liqueurs, though quite different, are just as appealing, and when you make them yourself you can give them an added dimension of flavor with the addition of an herb or two. A bit of ginger in pear brandy gives it a pleasant warmth; scented geraniums add a delicate nuance to fruits, as do any of the lemony herbs or the scented basils.

In Europe, owners of small restaurants and thoughtful hosts often offer guests a glass of

◟ Herbal liqueurs are made by adding herbs, fruits, spices, and sugar to vodka, then letting the ingredients steep while the flavors blend and mellow.

~ **Warm up a cold afternoon by stirring a little Chocolate Mint Liqueur into a cup of hot chocolate.**

their own after-dinner brandy. Made from fruit and a local brandy and served icy cold, they are a splendid ending to any dinner and a charming custom to take as your own.

Making these delicious drinks is a simple matter, but most require a bit of time to steep, so plan ahead. Since they continue to age and mellow in the refrigerator for at least six to eight months once they've been opened, you can make a selection to offer guests or to flavor desserts and sauces. Put them in pretty bottles you've collected at yard sales and flea markets all through the year, then when the holidays roll around you'll have some wonderful presents for deserving friends.

Most liqueurs are made in the same way: the fruits and/or herbs and spices are steeped in alcohol (generally vodka, since we don't have local brandies) for 2 to 4 weeks. For greater variety, you might want to substitute brandy or white rum or add some brandy or white wine to the vodka. To make sure your liqueurs are really fine, use the best ingredients and only glass or ceramic containers: metal and plastic add unwanted flavors of their own. Always steep, age, and store the liqueurs in a cool, dark spot unless otherwise noted and label and date them so you know exactly what you have and when they need to be filtered or bottled.

After steeping, the liquid is strained and filtered. To get really sparkling clear liquids, filter them through a coffee filter or a double layer of fine cheesecloth. At this point a simple syrup is added. If you do this gradually, tasting as you go, you can control the degree of sweetness, which will vary according to the sweetness of the fruit. It is wise to age liqueurs another week or two before bottling and using. Alternately, the sugar can be added in the beginning and the bottle shaken daily for a few days until the sugar has completely dissolved. The only drawback to this method is that it is more difficult to control the sweetness. If you want a fuller, more commercial consistency, add a teaspoon of glycerine (available at the pharmacy) before the final bottling.

Put the liqueurs in spotlessly clean and tightly sealed bottles for the final aging. If any residue develops as they age, refilter. Once the liqueurs are opened, store them in the refrigerator.

And don't forget: these intensely flavored liqueurs can add a nice dash to many recipes. Stir them into mousses, fruit salads and compotes, or sauces; blend them into vanilla ice cream or whipped cream for instant flavor; use them to sauce ice creams or sorbets; or add them to marinades or basting sauces for duck, chicken, or pork.

The following recipes represent a variety of tastes and methods, but you can combine different fruits, use dried fruits or herbs if fresh ones are not available, be adventuresome with seeds and spices. In general, for 4 cups of vodka you will need 1 to 3 cups of sugar; the amount will vary according to the fruits or herbs and personal preference.

～ BELOW: **Stir Rosemary Orange Liqueur into softened vanilla ice cream and refreeze in** scooped-out orange shells for an easy but elegant dessert. OVERLEAF: **For an interesting change of taste and extra kick use Rose Geranium Raspberry Liqueur instead of Cassis in a Kir Royale.**

ROSE GERANIUM RASPBERRY LIQUEUR

4 half pints raspberries
1 cup rose geranium leaves
4 cups vodka
½ cup white wine
1 cup sugar
½ cup water

Combine the berries, geranium leaves, vodka, and wine in a large jar with a tight-fitting cover. Place in a cool, dark place to steep for 1 month. Crush the berries slightly with a wooden spoon or potato masher and steep for another 4 days. Strain the liquid, pressing as much juice as possible from the berries, then filter. Boil the sugar and water together in a small saucepan until the sugar is dissolved; cool, then gradually stir into the liqueur, tasting as you go. When the liqueur has reached the desired level of sweetness, bottle and age for an additional 3 weeks in a cool, dark place.

MAKES ABOUT 1 1/2 QUARTS

Note: Amounts will vary according to the ripeness of the fruits and quantity of ingredients used.

❧ **Offering an assortment of herbal liqueurs is a delightful way to end a festive dinner.**

Variations

GINGER BERRY LIQUEUR: Use 1 pint strawberries and 2 half pints raspberries, and replace the rose geranium with 2 tablespoons candied ginger.

LEMON BERRY LIQUEUR: Use 1 pint strawberries and 2 half pints raspberries and substitute lemon geranium or lemon verbena for the rose geranium.

LIME THYME LIQUEUR: Use the zest from 6 well-washed limes, increase the sugar to 2 cups, water to 1 cup, and replace the rose geranium with 2 cloves and 2 sprigs fresh thyme or 1 teaspoon dried.

PEAR GINGER LIQUEUR: Use the juice from 8 very ripe pears (about 4 cups), increase the sugar to 2 cups, water to 1 cup, and replace the rose geranium with a 2-inch piece of fresh ginger root, peeled and sliced.

APRICOT THYME LIQUEUR: Use 1 pound dried apricots, substitute brandy for the wine, and use ¼ cup fresh lemon thyme or regular thyme or sage instead of the rose geranium.

ROSEMARY ORANGE LIQUEUR: Use 1 cup kumquats pricked with a fork or the zest of 1 orange in place of the berries, 6 small sprigs of rosemary instead of the rose geranium, and increase the sugar to 2 cups, water to 1 cup. Steep in the sun for 1 day before setting in a cool, dark place.

PINEAPPLE GINGER LIQUEUR: Use white rum in place of vodka, 4 cups cubed pineapple instead of berries, and 2 tablespoons candied ginger and ¼ cup orange mint or lime balm instead of rose geranium.

CHOCOLATE MINT LIQUEUR: Use ⅔ cup unsweetened cocoa in place of the berries; substitute ¾ cup tightly packed peppermint leaves for the rose geranium.

LEMON VERBENA LIQUEUR

½ cup lemon verbena leaves, tightly
    packed
1 5-inch strip of lemon zest (optional)
4 cups vodka or brandy
2 cups sugar

Place the lightly bruised lemon verbena leaves, the lemon zest if using, and the vodka or brandy in a large jar with a tight-fitting lid. Steep for 2 days, then add the sugar. Steep for 2 more weeks, shaking vigorously once or twice a day to dissolve the sugar, then strain and filter. Transfer the liqueur to bottles and age an additional 2 weeks before using.

MAKES ABOUT 1 QUART

Variations

TARRAGON LIQUEUR: Use 1 cup tightly packed tarragon sprigs in place of the lemon verbena, increase the sugar to 3 cups, and add ½ vanilla bean, split, in place of the lemon zest.

MINT LIQUEUR: Use 1 cup tightly packed peppermint leaves in place of the lemon verbena; omit the zest.

For a liqueur with an unexpectedly exotic taste, combine sweetly fragrant rose petals with the spiciness of nutmeg and cloves.

ROSE LIQUEUR: Use 3 cups fragrant unsprayed rose petals in place of the lemon verbena, and 2 cloves, a pinch of nutmeg, and 1 tablespoon rose water for the zest. Reduce the sugar to 1 cup.

THYME FLOWER LIQUEUR: Use 4 cups lightly packed thyme flowers in place of the lemon verbena; omit the zest.

CARNATION LIQUEUR: Use 1 cup tightly packed pink carnations, white heel removed, in place of the lemon verbena. Replace the lemon zest with 1 cinnamon stick and 1 clove. Reduce the sugar to 1 cup.

COFFEE ANISE LIQUEUR

½ pound coffee, coarsely ground
2 cups sugar
2 tablespoons aniseed
½ vanilla bean, split
4 cups vodka

Gently heat the ground coffee in a heavy pan over a low flame until it begins to release its aroma. Place the roasted coffee, sugar, aniseed, and vanilla in the bottom of a large jar with a tight-fitting lid and pour the vodka over them. Steep for 1 week, shaking frequently to help dissolve the sugar. Filter and bottle. Age an additional 2 weeks before using.

MAKES ABOUT 1 QUART

Fasten a wax paper collar around a 1½-quart soufflé dish, then lightly oil the dish.

Puree the berries in a food processor. Strain through cheesecloth into a small bowl to remove the seeds, then stir in the liqueur. Set aside.

Place the egg whites in a large bowl and beat until foamy. Gradually add the sugar, beating constantly, and continue to beat until the whites are thick and shiny and hold a peak. Carefully fold the berry mixture into the whipped cream, then fold in the egg whites. Pour the soufflé into the prepared dish and place in the freezer until the mixture begins to thicken, about 45 minutes to an hour. Remove from the freezer, stir in the ginger snap crumbs, and return to the freezer until frozen through, approximately 4 hours or overnight.

To serve, remove the collar from the dish and garnish as desired.

SERVES 8 TO 10

FROZEN GINGER BERRY SOUFFLE

A rich but light ending to any meal.

    2 pints strawberries or raspberries
    ⅓ cup Ginger Berry Liqueur
        (page 118)
    2 egg whites
    ½ cup sugar
    2 cups heavy cream, whipped
    ¾ cup large ginger snap crumbs
        Candied flowers, whipped cream,
        and/or berries for garnish (optional)

❧ ABOVE: **The spicy fragrance of pinks is reflected in the cinnamony liqueur made from their rosy petals.**
RIGHT: **Herbal berry liqueur intensifies the flavor of this iced mousse, especially helpful when berries are out-of-season.**

HERB WINES

When a flavorful herb is added to a decent bottle of wine and allowed to steep for a day or two, the results are delightful. Undoubtedly the best known of these herbal wines is the traditional May wine flavored with refreshing fresh woodruff, but many other herbs can be used. In France wine is often enhanced with fruit; the addition of herbs improves the flavor even more. Use the herbs sparingly, and consider the flavor of the fruit in choosing them. Serve these tasty wines icy cold on a hot afternoon with or without a dash of soda, or offer them as a delightful alternative to an aperitif before dinner.

SIMPLE HERB WINE

1 fifth dry white wine (or try a light red or rosé for a change of pace)
3 to 4 herb sprigs (lemon balm, rosemary, basil, rose petals, lemon verbena, angelica, bay, mint, tarragon, etc.)

Steep the herbs in the wine overnight in a cool, dark place. (Roses may need to be steeped for as long as 2 weeks to obtain a distinctive rose flavor.) Filter before serving.

MAKES 1 FIFTH

CHAMOMILE WINE

4 cups red or white wine
¼ cup dried chamomile flowers or ½ cup fresh
1 tablespoon orange peel
1 teaspoon lemon peel
3 tablespoons brown sugar

Place all the ingredients in a glass jar with a tight-fitting top and steep in a cool, dark place for 1 week. Filter and bottle.

MAKES ABOUT 1 QUART

∾ **Full-bodied Chamomile Wine is an excellent accompaniment to cheese.**

ORANGE MINT WINE

4 cups dry white wine
¼ cup sugar
½ cup brandy
Zest of 2 oranges
¼ cup orange or regular mint

Combine the wine and sugar in a non-aluminum pot and bring to a boil. Remove from the heat immediately, stir to dissolve the sugar, and cool to tepid. Put the orange zest and the mint in a large glass jar with a tight-fitting lid and pour the brandy and the wine mixture over them. Steep in a cool, dark place for 2 days and filter before using. If desired, add a fresh piece of zest and a sprig of mint to the bottle. This wine will keep for 3 months in the refrigerator.

MAKES ABOUT 1 QUART

Variations

RASPBERRY BALM WINE: Use 1 pint of raspberries and ¼ cup of lemon balm in place of the orange zest and mint.

SPICY PEACH WINE: Substitute 6 ripe peaches, peeled and pitted, for the orange zest and ¼ cup cinnamon basil for the mint. Simmer the peaches in the wine for 10 minutes.

ROSY SAGE APERITIF

1 bottle rosé wine
1 cup vodka, brandy, or white wine
3 small sprigs fresh sage
¼ cup honey

Place the wine, vodka or brandy, and sage in a glass jar with a tight-fitting lid. Steep in a cool, dark place for 2 weeks. Filter, stir in the honey, and pour into a bottle with a tight fitting cork. Store in a cool, dark place.

MAKES ABOUT 1 QUART

〜 OPPOSITE: **Orange wine, popular in the south of France, is even more delicious with a sprig of mint.** BELOW: **Raspberry Balm Wine is wonderfully refreshing on a summer afternoon.**

MRS. T'S ELDERFLOWER CORDIAL

This old-fashioned, non-alcoholic shrub has been a favorite in Caroline Collis's family for many years. It can only be made when the elderflowers are ripe in June, but this recipe supplies enough refreshment for a whole summer. Unopened, the cordial will keep for 1 year.

5½ cups water
9 pounds sugar
1 teaspoon citric acid (available at the pharmacy)
10 lemons, thinly sliced
20 elderflower heads in full bloom

In a large stockpot, heat the water, sugar, and citric acid. When the sugar is melted and the water is simmering, add the sliced lemons and the elderflower heads. Simmer for 5 minutes, then remove from the heat.

Cool, cover, and let stand at room temperature for 48 hours. Strain. Pour into sterilized bottles and seal. To serve, dilute with water to taste and pour over ice.

MAKES ABOUT 10 QUARTS

༚ **Poaching peaches in Spicy Peach Wine heightens the flavor of the fruit. Serve with cinnamon basil and cinnamon ice cream for added zip.**

PEACHES POACHED IN SPICY PEACH WINE

The spiciness of cinnamon basil is a nice complement to the sweetness of ripe peaches.

2 cups Spicy Peach Wine (page 127)
1 cup sugar
4 ripe peaches, washed
1 pint vanilla ice cream
1 tablespoon ground cinnamon
8 sprigs cinnamon basil for garnish

Place the wine, sugar, and peaches in a saucepan and bring to a boil over medium heat. Turn the heat down and poach, covered, until the peaches are just tender, about 10 minutes. Drain and cool the peaches, reserving the wine. When the peaches are cool enough to handle, carefully remove the skin, halve and pit the peaches, and place them in a bowl with the reserved wine.

An hour or two before serving, soften the ice cream and beat in the cinnamon. Return to the freezer. To serve, place 2 peach halves in each dish with a little of the syrup and spoon some cinnamon ice cream on top. Garnish with cinnamon basil leaves.

SERVES 4

HERBAL TEAS

Man has probably been drinking herbal infusions for pleasure as well as their healthful benefits ever since he discovered fire and was able to make hot water to extract the tasty and beneficial oils from the plants he gathered. Although herbal brews were once the province of health food stores and knowledgeable herbalists, as more and more people have discovered their delicate flavors and delightful aromas, their popularity has soared. These infusions have the added advantages of being calorie and caffeine free and often filled with vitamins and minerals. Moreover, the natural theraputic effects of herbs can lift your spirits, calm your nerves, help lull you to sleep, soothe your stomach, or even ease the misery of a cold.

At one time even the most devoted Chinese tea drinkers were so enamoured of sage tea, they traded many times the weight of precious Chinese tea for European sage. However, those accustomed to coffee can be disappointed by these teas' mild flavor. It may take time to atune your palate to the subtlety of herbs like chamomile, but try adding a sprig or two of a flavorful herb such as lemon verbena or rosemary to ordinary tea, and you'll soon find yourself enjoying the herbal versions. Cinnamon, cloves, and dried citrus rind can be added for extra zest, and honey will add a lovely sweetness.

The flowers and leaves, the seeds, or even the roots, bark, or stems of many herbs can be used for tea. Flowers, leaves, crushed seeds, and powdered herbs give up their flavor easily and are generally brewed by pouring boiling water over the herbs in the proportion of 1 cup water to 1 teaspoon dried or 1 tablespoon fresh herbs, a bit stronger if you are planning to serve it over ice. Cover the pot to prevent the aromatic steam from escaping and let the infusion steep from 3 to 10 minutes, depend-

~ **Indulge in the soothing ritual of steeping herbal tea in a pleasing antique teapot.**
OPPOSITE: **Afternoon Tea combines the natural tang of hibiscus and rosehips with the sweetness of orange.**

∿ Ingredients for tea making include dried linden leaves and flowers, hibiscus blossoms, lemon verbena, and rose hips.

ing on the herb. If you want a stronger flavor, use more herbs, because longer steeping may bring out a bitter flavor. Or put some fresh herbs and water in a clear glass jar and set it in the sun to "brew" on warm summer days.

Barks and roots need more coaxing to give up their oils so they are brewed as a decoction using the same ratio of ingredients. Put the herbs in cool water, bring them to the simmering point, then simmer, covered, for about 15 minutes.

For convenience, mix up large quantities of your favorite blends and store them in tightly closed glass jars in a cool, dark cupboard. Use dried ingredients, stored separately, to create variations. You'll find that mint, chamomile, linden, and lemon verbena mix well with most other herbs.

A GLOSSARY OF TEA HERBS

- *Aniseed.* Licorice flavor. Nerve soothing, sleep inducing, digestive, breath sweetener.
- *Basil.* Spicy. Promotes alertness, eases motion and morning sickness.
- *Bee balm.* Minty. Sleep inducing, relieves headaches and nausea.
- *Borage.* Mild cucumber flavor. Exhilarating; high in calcium and potassium.
- *Caraway seeds.* Refreshing. Digestive.
- *Chamomile.* Fruity aroma. Relaxing, aids digestion and nausea.
- *Catnip.* Minty. Sedative, lots of vitamin C.

- *Dill seeds.* Eases colic pains, mild tranquilizer.
- *Fennel seeds.* Anise flavor. Warm and stimulating, eases colic, diuretic.
- *Ginger.* Pungent. Stimulating, aids digestion.
- *Hibiscus.* Tangy citrus flavor. Sweetens stomach and breath.
- *Hops.* Bitter. Calming. Sedative, relieves hangover headaches.
- *Lavender blossom.* Sweet, exotic flavor. Relieves fatigue.
- *Lemon balm.* Lemony. Counteracts stress, soothes nerves.
- *Lemon grass.* Mild diuretic.
- *Lemon verbena.* Distinctly lemony flavor. Mild sedative.
- *Linden.* Mildly sweet. Tranquilizing, soothes nerves, indigestion.
- *Marjoram.* Pungent. Calming.
- *Mints.* Aids digestion, relieves nausea and flatulence, sweetens breath.
- *Orange blossom.* Sedative.
- *Parsley.* Rich in vitamin C, natural diuretic, more like a broth.
- *Rose geranium.* Spicy rose flavor.
- *Rose hips.* Slight citrus flavor. Rich in vitamins C and A.
- *Rosemary.* Aromatic. Good for nervous headaches.
- *Sage.* Pungent. Aids digestion, relieves sore throats.
- *Thyme.* Spicy, pungent. Eases tension headaches, sore throats.

If you want to substitute fresh herbs in any of the following recipes, triple the amount.

Chamomile and dried orange peel nestle among Chris's collection of antique tea pots.

ZESTY LEMON TEA

Delicious hot or iced.

¼ cup dried lemon balm leaves
2 tablespoons dried lemon thyme
  leaves
¼ cup dried lemon verbena leaves
¼ cup dried lemon geranium leaves
2 tablespoons dried lemon grass leaves
1 tablespoon dried lavender blossoms

ENOUGH FOR ABOUT
30 CUPS

SPICY TEA

A lovely pick-me-up on cold afternoons that's equally good iced.

¼ cup dried lemon verbena
¼ cup dried chamomile
¼ cup dried orange peel
2 tablespoons dried rosemary
1 3-inch cinnamon stick, crushed

ENOUGH FOR ABOUT
30 CUPS

AFTERNOON TEA

A flavorful blend to enjoy when you need a break.

¼ cup dried hibiscus flowers
½ cup dried chamomile
2 tablespoons dried rose hips
1 tablespoon dried orange peel
1 3-inch cinnamon stick, crushed

ENOUGH FOR ABOUT
30 CUPS

THERAPEUTIC TEA

Whenever a cold threatens, I brew myself a cup of this bracing tea. Whether or not the naturally antiseptic properties of thyme, the throat-soothing sage, and energizing ginger actually help bring about a cure, they certainly do make me feel better.

⅓ cup dried thyme
⅓ cup dried leaf sage
⅓ cup powdered ginger

ENOUGH FOR ABOUT
30 CUPS

∽ Iced Zesty Lemon Tea provides
pleasant refreshment on a hot day.

DIGESTIVE TEA

This is the tea to drink when you've eaten too much.

2 tablespoons dried thyme
2 tablespoons dried rosemary
¼ cup dried mint
2 tablespoons aniseed
¼ cup lemon verbena

ENOUGH FOR ABOUT
30 CUPS

BEDTIME TEA

Try drinking a cup of this tea when you want a good night's sleep.

¼ cup dried chamomile
¼ cup dried linden leaves
2 tablespoons dried mint
1 tablespoon dried orange blossoms
  (optional)
2 tablespoons lemon verbena

ENOUGH FOR ABOUT
25 CUPS

LEMON GRANITA

A refreshing finale for a heavy meal.

4 cups Zesty Lemon Tea (page 135)
1½ cups sugar
2½ cups fresh lemon juice
  Lemon herbs, lemon zest, or berries
  for garnish

Combine the tea and sugar in a large non-aluminum saucepan and stir to begin dissolving the sugar. Place over medium heat and cook, stirring, just until the liquid comes to a boil and the sugar is dissolved. Remove the lemon syrup from the heat and allow it to cool completely. Stir in the lemon juice and pour the mixture into a shallow glass or enamel dish. Place the dish in the freezer for 5 hours, stirring thoroughly every hour. After 5 hours, pack the granita in a bowl or decorative mold and refreeze. Unmold before serving and garnish with herbs, zest, or berries.

SERVES 10 TO 12

~ Icy cold Lemon Granita garnished with borage flowers, LEFT AND RIGHT, is a light but delicious ending to a summer luncheon.

SOURCE DIRECTORY

The directory that follows offers a list of shops that specialize in herbal vinegars, blends, and other herbal foods, as well as a listing of sources for herbal plants and seeds. Many shops sell both herbal products and herb gardening supplies; these are noted with an asterisk*. Those that sell via mail order have the notation (MO). Stores vary widely in their hours; it is therefore wise to check by telephone before visiting the shops listed.

HERBAL FOODS

ANGELICA'S
147 First Avenue
New York, NY 10003
(212) 529-4335 (MO)

APHRODISIA
282 Bleecker Street
New York, NY 10014
(212) 838-6878 (MO)

THE APPLE FARM
18501 Greenwood Road
Philo, CA
(707) 895-2333

CASADOS FARMS
P. O. Box 1269
San Juan Pueblo, NM 87566
(505) 852-2433 (MO)

CRICKET HILL HERB FARM LTD.
Glen Street
Rowley, MA 01969
(508) 948-2818 * (MO)

EMELIE TOLLEY'S HERB BASKET
P. O. Box 1332
Southampton, NY 11969
(MO)

FINES HERBES
4 Leonard Street
New York, NY 10013
(212) 334-1230 (MO)
(Fresh cut herbs)

FOX HILL FARM
443 West Michigan Avenue
P. O. Box 9
Parma, MI 49269
(517) 531-3179 * (MO)

FREDERICKSBURG HERB FARM
402 Whitney
P.O. Drawer 927
Fredericksburg, TX 78624
(512) 997-8615 * (MO)

THE HERB CUPBOARD
Box 375 Route 163
Fort Plain, NY 13339
(518) 993-2363 * (MO)

THE HERB GARDEN
109 North Montgomery Street
Ojai, CA 93023
(805) 646-7065 *

HERB GATHERING, INC.
5742 Kenwood Avenue
Kansas City, MO 64110
(816) 523-2653

HERB HOLLOW
Safford Road
East Otto, NY 14729
(716) 257-5105 * (MO)

THE HERB HOUSE CATALOG
340 Grove Street
Bluffton, OH 45817
(419) 358-7189 (MO)

THE HERB PATCH, INC.
Concord, MA
Also Belmont Center, MA
(617) 369-1948 * *or*
(508) 263-2405

THE HERB AND SPICE COLLECTION
Box 118
Norway, IA 52318
(800) 365-4372 (MO)

HIDDEN HOLLOW HERBIARY
N88 W. 18407 Duke Street
Menomonea Falls, WI 53051
(414) 251-5061 * (MO)

IT'S ABOUT THYME
729 FM 1626
P. O. Box 878
Manchaca, TX 78652
(512) 280-1192

**Maria Price's Willow Oak
Flower and Herb Farm**
8109 Telegraph Road
Severn, MD 21144
(301) 551-2237 * (MO)

**Meadowbrook Herb
Garden**
Route 138
Wyoming, RI 02898
(401) 539-7603 * (MO)

Naomi's Herbs
11 Housatonic Street
Lenox, MA 01240
(413) 637-0616 * (MO)

Patti's Herbs
Route 1, Box 31J
Pearsall, TX 78061
(512) 334-3944 (MO)
(Fresh cut herbs)

Pickety Place
Nutting Hill Road
Mason, NH 03048
(603) 878-1151 * (MO)

Rathdowney Ltd.
3 River Street
Bethel, VT 05032
(802) 234-9928 (MO)

Red Saffron
3009 16th Avenue South
Minneapolis, MN 55407
(612) 724-3686
(Mail order only)

The Rosemary House, Inc.
120 South Market Street
Mechanicsburg, PA 17055
(717) 697-5111 * (MO)

Sassafrass Herbs, Inc.
P. O. Box 50192
Nashville, TN 37203

Stillridge Herb Farm
10370 Route 99
Woodstock, MD 21163
(301) 465-8348 * (MO)

**Strawberry Meadow
Herb Farm, Inc.**
RFD #3 Box 3689
Pleasant Street
Pittsfield, NH 03263
(603) 435-6132 * (MO)

Tea Thyme Herb Farm
P.O. Box 304
Denver in the Catskills
Denver, NY 12421
(607) 326-7776

Timber Rock Farms
R. D. #2 Box 290E
Emporium, PA 15834
(814) 486-7685 (MO)

Woodland Herb Farm
7741 No. Manitou Trail W.
Northport, MI 49670
(616) 386-5081 * (MO)

SEEDS AND PLANTS

Alloway Gardens
Route 1, Box 183
Littlestown, PA 17340
(717) 359-4548 *

Antique Rose Emporium
Route 5, Box 143
Brenham, TX 77833
(409) 836-9051 (MO)

Caprilands Herb Farm
Silver Street
Coventry, CT 06238
(203) 742-7244 * (MO)

Catnip Acres Herb Farm
67 Christian Street
Oxford, CT 06483
(203) 888-5649

Cedarbrook Herb Farm
986 Sequim Avenue South
Sequim, WA 98382
(206) 683-7733 * (MO)

Companion Plants
7247 North Coolville Ridge
Athens, OH 45701
(614) 592-4643 (MO)

**Gilbertie's Herb
Gardens, Inc.**
Sylvan Lane
Westport, CT 06880
(203) 227-4175

The Farmhouse
10,000 N.W. 70th Avenue
Grimes, IA 50111
(515) 986-3628

The Flowery Branch
P. O. Box 1330
Flowery Branch, GA 30542
(Mail order only)

Four-Leaf Clover Herb Farm
R.D. #1 Ridge Road
Natrona Heights, PA 15065
(412) 224-5125 *

Goodwin Creek Gardens
154 1/2 Oak Street
Ashland, OR 97520
(505) 488-3308 * (MO)

GOURMET GARDENS HERB FARM
14 Banks Town Road
Weaverville, NC 28787
(704) 658-0766 *

GREENFIELD HERB GARDEN
Depot & Harrison
P. O. Box 437
Shipshewana, IN 46565
(219) 768-7110 * (MO)

HEARD'S COUNTRY GARDENS
14391 Edwards Street
Westminster, CA 92683
(714) 894-2444 *

THE HERB FARM
13182 Pierce Road
Hagerstown, IN 47346
(3127) 886-5193 *

THE HERBFARM
Box 116
Wilkins, OR 97544
(206) 784-2222 * (MO)

LE JARDIN DU GOURMET
West Danville, VT 05873 (MO)

**LEWIS MOUNTAIN HERBS
& EVERLASTINS**
2345 Street Rt. 247
Manchester, OH 45144
(513) 549-2484

LILY OF THE VALLEY HERB FARM
3969 Fox Avenue
Minerva, OH 44657
(216) 862-3920 * (MO)

LOST PRAIRIE HERB FARM
805 Kienas Road
Kalispell, MT 59901
(406) 756-7742 (MO)

LUCIA'S GARDEN
2213 Portsmouth Street
Houston, TX 77098
(713) 523-6494

NICHOL'S GARDEN NURSERY
1190 North Pacific Highway
Albany, OR 97321
(503) 928-9280 * (MO)

THE OLD GREENHOUSE
1415 Devil's Backbone Road
Cincinnati, OH 45233
(513) 941-0337

OTTO RICHTER & SONS, LTD.
Box 26
Goodwood, Ontario
Canada, LOC 1AO
(416) 640-6677 (MO)

PECONIC RIVER HERB FARM
310-C River Road
Calverton, NY 11933
(516) 369-0058

PLANTS OF THE SOUTHWEST
1812 Second Street
Santa Fe, NM 87501
(505) 983-1548 (MO)

RASLAND FARM
NC 82 at US 13
Godwin, NC 28344
(919) 567-2705 * (MO)

ROSES OF YESTERDAY AND TODAY
802 Brown's Valley Road
Watsonville, CA 95076
(408) 724-2755 (MO)

SANDY MUSH HERB NURSERY
Route #2, Surrett Cove Road
Leicester, NC 28748
(704) 683-2014 (MO)

SHADY HILL GARDENS
803 Walnut Street
Batavia, IL 60510
(312) 879-5665 (MO)

SHEPHERD'S GARDEN SEEDS
7389 W. Zayante Road
Felton, CA 95018
(408) 335-5311 (MO)

TAYLOR'S HERB GARDENS, INC.
1535 Lone Oak Road
Vista, CA 92084
(619) 727-3485 (MO)

T. DE BAGGIO HERBS
923 North Ivy Street
Arlington, VA 22201
(703) 243-2498

WELL-SWEEP HERB FARM
317 Mt. Bethal Road
Port Murray, NJ 07865
(201) 852-5390 * (MO)

WOLF HILL FARM
30 Jericho Hill Road
Southborough, MA 01772
(508) 485-5087

WOODLANDERS, INC.
1128 Colleton Avenue
Aiken, SC 29801
(804) 648-7522
(Mail order only)

**WRENWOOD OF
BERKELEY SPRINGS**
Route 4, Box 361
Berkeley Springs, WV 25411
(304) 258-3071 * (MO)